A DEER IN THE HEADLIGHTS

Losing My Freedom

Roland "Spanky" Macher

A Deer in the Headlights
Losing My Freedom

ISBN 978-0-9988090-9-0

Published by:
Slumlord Millionaire LLC

Contents

Introduction

I'm sure you never thought you would be looking from the inside out. I know that never in my wildest dreams did I expect to be here, not ever. Maybe you grew up like I did, knowing right from wrong, having some core values in place. Or maybe you didn't. Either way, not too many people are planning their futures around going into prison, are they? I know I didn't. Yet, it happened to me and it could happen to you. This book shares my memoires, experiences and gives you a birds-eye glimpse at what you may expect. Of course, each county jail, reformatory, federal prison, or private prison looks differently, the people inside those walls may (or may not) behave differently, but the model is relatively the same across the board.

I've also included some articles of interest, photos, and must-have information that could potentially assist you when it's time to go home.

Tributes

I would like to thank my friend Dallas who faithfully stood by me as I served my time.

I am dedicating this book to the guys that I was able to share 21 months of my life with.

Smilez, Biz, Warren, Tracy, Fresh, Connor, Dave, Kevin, Andy, Kevin *2*, Billie and Juice, who were on the softball team with me. Thank you K.C., Dean, Danny, Drew, Rudy, Shea, Warren, Mills, Lam, Hobo, Juice, Greek, Black, Bud, and John, Freddy, Matt, Alberto, Tony, Ed and Bud, as well as the many others that I connected with while in camp Hazelton.

Introduction to the Camp

Some Information About My New Home

USP HAZELTON is located in Bruceton Mills, West Virginia. It has two facilities, one which is a high-security US Penitentiary and the other which is considered a minimum-security satellite camp. There is also another facility that is titled a medium-security federal correctional institution with a secured female facility that is located on the grounds.

The Bureau of Federal Prisons was established in 1930 to provide more progressive and humane care for federal inmates, to professionalize the prison service, and to ensure consistent and centralized administration of federal prisons.[1] Or so they say...

Here's what their mission statement looks like on their website:

It is the mission of the Federal Bureau of Prisons to protect society by confining offenders in the controlled environments of prisons and community-based facilities that are safe, humane, cost-efficient, and appropriately secure, and that provide work and other self-improvement opportunities to assist offenders in becoming law-abiding citizens. [2]

---

[1] https://www.bop.gov/about/

[2] https://www.bop.gov/about/agency/agency_pillars.jsp

The Bureau of Prisons website is pretty impressive. A good website developer must have landed a hefty contract with the Government. Here is the link: https://www.bop.gov/. As you can see, it gives an inmate and his/her family members some resources to explore what to expect as far as mailing items to an inmate, visitations, and a conglomeration of other items of interest.

True Story

This is a true story or at least the good parts are! For some, this cavalcade of tragic anecdotes is based on real facts, some of which will be sad, and others rude awakenings. It is necessary and long overdue to present the wake-up call for the citizens of America. There have been many similar wake-up calls in the past, but this country continues to sleep through them.

For decades, the justice system in this country, on a whole, has been begging for an enema. Specifically, it's time to cleanse the obscene quagmire of its wrongful criminal prosecutions. Many of the activities that have been taking place for over a century are an injustice to those who are still breathing.

As uncomfortable as this may sound, the delay in providing this enema has been due to not knowing exactly where to make the insertion for the quickest and most effective results. Time is now a factor and the location has been confirmed.

<u>Uncle Sam's Magic Carpet</u> is a true, riveting, and disturbing satirical exposure of wrongful convictions, indictments, and sentencing. This conglomeration has created a holocaust of injustice, which has been festering for years within the country's deteriorating justice system.

The criminal justice system produces countless erroneous determinations of guilt or innocence. With the impact of social media outlets, how is it possible for someone to receive a fair and impartial jury trial? Yes, sometimes honest mistakes happen, but more often than not, so do dishonest mistakes. The focus herein is on the latter. More people than imaginable are sent through this discriminating judgment process and are subsequently handed punishment. Perhaps the system tends to circle its wagons in the time of need. Law enforcement officers stick together, prosecutors mobilize to ward off all legal challenges, and judges tend to uphold the actions of other judges. These tendencies make it all the more difficult for all wrongly convicted individuals to prove their innocence. The system criminalizes ordinary conduct through accordion-like criminal statutes, and because of that, in part, the system has broken down. Was it intact to begin with? It's far easier to find someone guilty of something than it is to later determine that they are innocent. It's very likely that many of those innocent people who have been wrongly convicted, but not exonerated, will never receive their just vindication. They'll remain behind the walls of a state penitentiary, etc. It doesn't matter if there is decisive evidence that works in their favor, there is never enough time or resources to bring a case back to court. Don't get me wrong, it can still happen, but most likely not.

We should never come to the conclusion that the legal system in this country works, as we can see it doesn't. Take Nixon's war on drugs, for example. This policy was designed to reduce the activity of the drug trade and provide consequences for drug use. Instead, it impacted hundreds of thousands of black Americans, by structuring harsh sentences for drug crimes. Yet, a child rapist will spend less time behind bars than a big-time marijuana dealer.

Whatever happened to you are innocent until proven guilty? That's a key statement within itself. Instead of being innocent until you are proven guilty, people are deemed guilty before they even get to court. Our media has a huge hand in that. Many prosecutors should be charged and convicted of criminal misconduct, but how often does that happen? Instead, the public turns the other cheek and we get what we get.

Harold Clarke, Chief Justice of the Georgia Supreme Court once said: "We set our sights on the embarrassing target of mediocrity. I guess that means about halfway. And that raises a question, are we willing to put up with halfway justice? To my way of thinking one-half justice, means one-half injustice, and one-half injustice is no justice at all." [3]

Once inside the system, by way of incarceration, a person becomes invisible, forgotten, and exchanges a name for a number. Imprisonment for targeted

---

[3] State of Judiciary Speech to Legislator, January 12, 1994

and innocent victims is like a living death. Any imprisoned being becomes a lonely person, pitied by their family and friends. They're a scavenger of misery. Every convict is a lonesome cowboy riding his horse in the direction it's leading, regardless of who you connect with beyond the wall.

Wrongful prosecution of unintentional conduct gets twisted into felony charges that destroy many innocent people's lives and careers. Family members become pitted against one another. Friends may find themselves "persuaded by the government" to testify against you, even when their testimonies become less than honest. Even lawyers and their clients will turn on each other, just as doctors and their patients. How can society benefit when it is influenced by a reckless government, while they're claiming to be on a crusade against crime? In the meantime, they're preaching from lawbooks and using draconian techniques. These dark practices take place in the abuse of power.

The United States has become a country filled with sheep, speckled with wolves, and some of those wolves are dressed in sheep's clothing. Sheep stay with their flock and follow their shepherd without questioning where he is leading them. Sheep trust that the shepherd would never do anything to harm them, that he would always protect them from the wolves. The wolves, on the other hand, do not aimlessly follow a shepherd. In the darkness of the night, wolves howl, alerting the shepherd of their presence. Wolves question the shepherd and act in a way that forces the shepherd to question his decisions. The wolves in society challenge government regulations, reject government assistance and demand that the government recognize and protect their natural rights. They are rugged individuals that stand up for themselves and fight to protect themselves. Unfortunately, the majority of Americans are sheep.

Far too often, the Department of Justice, (DOJ) has successfully convinced the public through the corrupt media, that its prosecutors are actually cleaning up some of the hidden nests of corruption that exists within the system. Instead, they continue to reflect the threat that they pose to the nation. While this makes for some good conversation, it really lacks substance. Some reporters are readily accepting what the government tells us at face value. They must volunteer to dissect the government's claims of who killed who, or who committed a robbery, rape, or treason. The media needs to understand how and why the government determines how people have even broken the law. They need to examine what makes them criminals.

Nobody is suggesting that many of those who have been prosecuted are not criminals who have engaged in real crimes, defined by clear and reasonable laws. What is being scrutinized are the growing exceptions that are far too numerous to miss, and the burgeoning phenomenon of prosecuting the innocent on the basis of undecipherable statutes, and regulations that are too dangerous to ignore. Our justice system is troubled and broken. The media can assist in the process of repair by taking the time to investigate the realities of just how broken the system is. Too much has been swept under **<u>Uncle Sam's Magic Carpet</u>** for too long. American's do not realize how loud their voice can become. If they would just come together and let their anger be known. If friends and family members of wrongly convicted and incarcerated people would allow their voices to be heard, maybe it would make some impact.

The statistics are clear. Appeals and habeas corpus motions after incarceration are sad expressions of hope. When you are in prison, hope is the only comfort, you have in an imperfect condition. Let's look at 73-year-old Christopher Caswell's case. His story captures the crux of the injustice that takes place with shocking disbelief. He was clearly a victim of the government, whose story is particularly poignant.[4]

For several decades, there has been an on-again-off-again interest in the plight of wrongly convicted individuals in this country. This occurs when a high-profile case gets the attention of the public. The public receives a sprinkling of newspaper stories, spotty television exposure, and maybe even a fitful magazine article or two. To date, nothing significant has occurred to rectify the problem. The government wagons continue to be circled. There have been some outrage and cries that have actually helped a few people win their freedom, but the issues must be addressed at its roots to prevent wrongful convictions. I compare it to throwing a stone into a pond. The initial splash creates some large ripples, but the water quickly settles back to its original stillness, and the last disturbance is forgotten.

---

[4] https://www.vacourts.gov/courts/scv/amendments_tracked/rule_5_04_5_07_5_17a_5a_4_interlineated.pdf

The three most frequently uttered words that you will hear come from a wrongfully convicted person's mouth is, "win my freedom". Unfortunately, in confined settings, happy endings are rare exceptions. Part of the problem is the media outlets represent the world as black and white, good and bad, just as the adversary system of criminal law clings to Manichaean notions of innocence or guilt.

The real world is often gray, filled with many contradictions, and plagued by doubts. In some instances, sensational, erroneous, or news coverage leads to convictions. Gullible people believe everything they are told by the media.

How could anyone possibly foresee that these real-life tragic crime anecdotes collectively would be a prelude to the drama that is played out on the world's stage? Awareness is no longer an option.

The stories in **<u>Uncle Sam's Magic Carpet</u>** literally uncover and transport to the forefront the inner working of some of the most esteemed institutions of the United States. It was Norman Vincent Peale who said, "Imagination is the true magic carpet." If this is the case, Uncle Sam has volumes of it fossilizing in the form of distorted facts by way of inventiveness.

There is an efficient, volatile treatise that should enlighten everyone with the menacing, persistent inequities within this country's "Injustice System". It continues to fester and will blow up one day. Voltaire extended words of caution and concern when he said "It is dangerous to be right in matters on which the established authorities are wrong."[5] In doing so, we are microscopically revealing the treatment afforded on average citizens by prosecuting attorneys, defense attorneys, public defenders, the FBI, and even federal judges. There are clearly no isolated areas within the system that have escaped the infection and stench of the legal misconduct that is so severe and mind-boggling.

The malefactor is known as prosecutorial misconduct. It ulcerates within the country's justice system and continues to grow like fungus. It became discernible 100 years ago and the government has been using it like a carpenter uses a hammer ever since. Sadly, the government refuses to clean it up. The only time the government reacts to innocent people who are wrongly convicted and imprisoned or even executed for crimes they did not commit, is when it's called to their attention as acts of injustice. History teaches us that man is

---

[5] Spanky Macher

basically a psychopath. He never learns. History is cyclical; what goes around, comes around, full circle. It's like a tie, they never really go out of style, they may look a little different each year, but they don't go away.

Our government is too supercilious.

Prosecutorial misconduct materializes in murder cases on one end of the criminal spectrum and leads to mundane traffic violations on the other end of the spectrum. It's used as a fly swatter, only when necessary. Prosecutorial misconduct may be a new term for you, but it's sorely affecting thousands of innocent people accused of a crime in this country on a daily basis. It inhales friends and family like a vacuum cleaner inhales dust. Once the government targets its quarry, everyone who is involved with that individual becomes branded, like cattle, and are tagged as a "person of interest". They are used and abused until they get what they are looking for.

You may be surprised to learn that the government actually uses family members as bait to expedite convictions of their mark. With no compunction, the DOJ has badgered its targets with patented remarks like, "plead guilty or we will indict your wife", or "we will harass your children for the rest of their lives." The sick part of that is they will follow through with their threats and they get away with it. They can indict a cucumber if they want to. Surely you remember Bernard Madoff, the financier who bilked investors out of billions of dollars? Hells bells, his footprints to the "Big House" are still warm. The Madoff name is toxic.

Bernard Madoff was indeed punished and rightfully so. His son Mark Madoff committed suicide at the age of 46, primarily due to the continued harassment of personal persecution by the government. Yes, for the record, the government tortures innocent people by continuously harassing them. They go for your financial records, they track every move you make, they spy on your family, and it's impossible to make a move without that monkey on your back. This will continue as long as Americans overlook and excuse what is actually considered crimes committed by Uncle Sam. The sheep allow the deception of torture, which eventually leads to slaughter.

The systems have migrated from targeting crimes to targeting people. They create crimes and the rationalization that the individuals targeted are surely guilty. The government must consider that "progress". How do you argue with 100 years of this history? You almost can't prove otherwise.

I consider prosecutorial misconduct as being best described as a remedial disease, that isn't specific to prosecutors as the carriers, but others, such as the public defenders, defense attorneys, FBI agents, the CIA, forensic lab technicians, law enforcement officers, and of course judges. They all use a hammer when a protruding nail has reared its head. A hammer considers everything a nail that's in the arsenal. The DOJ condones its superman-like crusade against crime. Anyone affiliated with the DOJ is a carrier of prosecutorial misconduct, even if they're unaware of what's going on. It's kind of like all birds being carriers of parrot fever. Once a prosecutor targets an individual for a crime, especially when they seize assets, there is no going back, it's game on!

The prosecutor now has to provide evidence or create evidence to implicate that a crime has taken place. Victims have to be identified, witnesses probed, stories created to support the evidence, all pieces have to fit the system's puzzle. If those pieces don't fit, they determine a way to pound that circle into a square hole. The prosecutor always has the advantage, because they know the rules. Typically, the defendant is considered "blind" and must rely on his/her attorney like a "seeing-eye dog". The prosecutor transforms the bad lies into a plausible reality to ensure that justice will happen. They have to be willing to sacrifice their ethics and integrity to do so. That is if they have any, to begin with. Stories are created so that they stand up to the legal muster and justify the actions that need to be performed. Once that is fixed, the rest will fall into place. The house of cards is carefully constructed.

The problem with these conspiracies is self-evident to a prosecutor. The more people it takes to ignite the flame for this conduct, the harder it is to keep the deceit under control. Building a bomb for devious and destructive purposes is one thing, setting it off is something else. The DOJ continues to look the other way. Prosecutors are never punished for their criminal activity so they know they have nothing to lose.

Is it safe to say that not all people play misconduct all of the time or just some of the people do so all of the time? They all violate real laws, rules, and their own sanctions of code of ethics. Yet, most of them still function unscathed inside of the justice system, almost like refugees seeking asylum with their respective country's embassy.

Prosecutors enjoy the power they have to control potential life and death decisions or to ruin the lives and careers of others, as they preserve their own security within their careers. Most of this decision-making takes place behind closed doors and without scrutiny. Those prosecutors that participate in misconduct clearly show disrespect for the law, which is typically associated with criminals, not the men and women who prosecute them.

The United States Supreme Court has ruled that prosecutors are entitled to absolute immunity from harassing litigation that would divert time and attention from their official duties. Some of those who realize what's going on, morally question the wisdom of granting absolute immunity to prosecutors when they have violated an individual's constitutional rights. Nonetheless, the stigma of "prosecutorial misconduct" should be prolific with prosecutors, as the stigma of "felon" is to those who have been released from federal prisons.

A Pace University professor, Bennett Gersham, who specializes in prosecution issues, calls prosecutorial misconduct, "a serious cancer in our system of Justice." adding, "There is no check on prosecutorial misconduct, except for the prosecutor's own attitudes, beliefs, and inner morality".[6] Their philosophies reveal advanced thinking, it's very cerebral.

In New York, efforts to pass legislation holding prosecutors more accountable have failed. Their chief sponsor, Assemblyman, Sam Coleman of the 93rd District insists: "In most cases where an innocent person has ended up in jail, the prosecutor has been over-zealous. Don't forget, their job is to seek justice, not convictions. But district attorneys are arrogant people. I'd like to see them held more accountable".[7] Coleman wants to make prosecutors subject to a strict code enforced by an independent board, modeled after the system that governs judges. Most of lawmakers are afraid to cross paths with powerful prosecutors. The District Attorney's Association rules the roost. Coleman's suggestion is certainly a small step in the right direction. However, like all other genuine suggestions to curtail the power of prosecutors and all courtroom officials, it falls on deaf ears.

---

[6] Gresham, Bennett L., Pace University, Prosecutorial Misconduct, 1997.
[7] Coleman, Sam

Dozens of rules constrain prosecutors, but only on paper. The prohibitions against suppressing evidence, and knowingly using false evidence, are only two of them. Courts have established rules of a fair trial that over everything from the prosecutors of securing an indictment to what they can say during a trial closing argument. Prosecutors commit misconduct when they break those rules.

In addition, this misconduct might be knowingly discriminating against blacks during a jury selection, engaging in personal attacks towards a defense attorney, or destroying the credibility of a witness with questions containing false allegations. They may suggest jurors should infer guilt because a defendant didn't personally testify. These are the more obvious violations that prosecutors use and camouflage in many ways.

It is well documented; all victims of prosecutorial misconduct are permanently crippled by the actions of the government. Anyone of these victims could be your next-door neighbor, brother, or business colleague. It has been proven time and time again that numerous targeted people are innocent of any wrongdoings, yet their lives are compromised. You would be shocked to find out exactly how the DOJ handles these flagrant improprieties that deal with constitutional and civil rights.

The lesson is simple but clear. Anyone in this country can be targeted by the government for a crime, as well as a multitude of illogical reasons. With that being said, any one of these true stories could easily be your story. God, forbid!

When George W. Bush was President, he authorized a domestic surveillance program that the top legal advisors at the DOJ told him was illegal and unconstitutional. Bush insisted that eavesdropping on telephone calls and reading American citizens' emails was crucial to national security and the prevention of future terrorist attacks. The problem is the government doesn't just watch suspected terrorists but is spying on everyday people. This is a clear violation of our privacy. There are no guidelines defining who can be monitored. Guidelines are non-existent. As a result, innocent and law-abiding citizens of this country are being secretly monitored, robbed of their fundamental civil rights that are guaranteed in the Constitution of the United States of America.

The government continues to target people, with its primary mission to make them into criminals for various reasons. It is a simple way to pay back favors, "cooperating" entities, and an excellent permanent solution to destroy your enemies at home, just make them criminals!

George Orwell was the pen name for Eric Arthur Blair, a British novelist, and social critic. He became this through his novel, "**<u>1984</u>**", which by the way was published in 1949. The book is a frightening portrait of a totalitarian society that punishes love, destroys privacy, and distorts the truth. Sound familiar? There is a passage in this book that so aptly describes wrongful convictions in this country today, as manufactured by the DOJ, and prosecutors in particular.

"We shall crush you down to a point from which there is no coming back. Things will happen to you from which you could not recover, even if you lived a thousand years. Never again will you be capable of ordinary human feeling. Everything will be dead inside of you. Never again will you be capable of love, or friendship, or the joy of living, or laughter, or curiosity, or courage, or integrity. You will be hollow. We shall squeeze you empty, and then we shall fill you with ourselves".[8]

<u>Uncle Sam's Magic Carpet</u> briefly, but thoroughly, examines a number of specific cases in capsule form, a difficult task given the complexities of the events and issues involved. Concise accounts can never do justice to the sufferings endured by so many. Instead, they can reveal some common patterns and general characteristics that are critical to the problem. Collectively, they may provide insight into some of the causes and consequences of wrongful convictions. It is hoped that some of the humanity of those involved will come through.

While some of the names contained within this book are fictitious, solely at the discretion of the author, most of the names are real. It's the real people whose careers may be in jeopardy by the very actions as stated within these pages, and deservedly so. For entirely way too long, these people have been hiding under the safeguarding skirt of the DOJ. The game of hide-and-seek is over for violators of misconduct from police officers to judges. Their actions were swept under **<u>Uncle Sam's Magic Carpet</u>** and the carpet has now been located.

There are passages herein that will make you cry, scorn, and even laugh. Don't let any emotion you encounter distract you from the severity of the issues

---

[8] Spanky Macher

that you're going to discover. Sections of this book are readable and accurate because of the sources referenced accordingly.

You will soon see how vile prosecutorial misconduct can be, and how encompassing it is, as it affects the lives of many. Whether you're on the inside looking out or the outside looking in. You'll hopefully "feel" how the DOJ's and prison system's corrupt nature impacts so many different people and many other aspects of our world.

A wrongful conviction case serves as a paradigm of what goes on every day in the administration of justice. Often, the errors are simply not caught. Then there will be that one case that opens Pandora's Box, exposing all of the deep-seated issues, the widespread corruption, the inexcusable practices, and the systemic abuse. It's no wonder officials for at least 100 years have swept these areas of misconduct under **<u>Uncle Sam's Magic Carpet</u>**, where it fossilizes and fades away. Realistically, offices or even a full department could become implicated in some nasty accusations. Without damage control, you only can help but to wonder how many cases will explode or disintegrate.

Above all, wrongful convictions represent tragic and costly flaws in our system of justice and society. While these actions may go undetected, they are not invisible. They are certainly existent but not insignificant. It's as if they're right in front of your face but you can't see them. This is par for the course, after all, it's what they do.

Supreme Court Justice, Joseph Slavin reiterated, "The greatest crime of all times in a civilized society is an unjust conviction. It is truly a scandal, which reflects unfavorably on all of the participants in the criminal justice system. No one is entitled to a fair trial".

Conditions that affect the amount of crime vary from one country to another. Studies have shown that crime rates for both violent and property crime rose in most countries in the late 1900s. The FBI tracks the rate of violent crime per 100,000 inhabitants. Even though the rates of violent crime have been decreasing since 1990, the United States tops the prison population in the world.

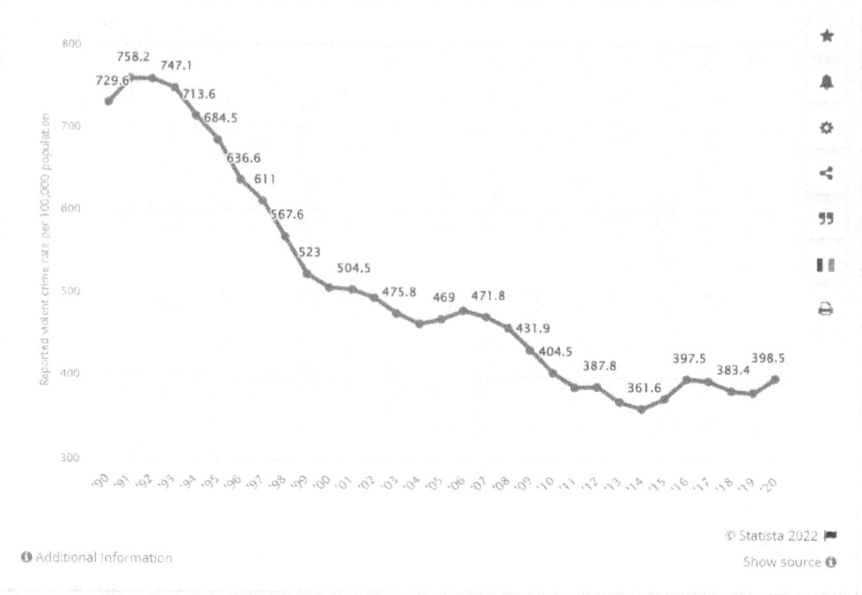

https://www.statista.com/statistics/191219/reported-violent-crime-rate-in-the-usa-since-1990

Through my research, I had found that those countries with higher rates of crime include the United States, China, Russia, and South Africa. Lower crime rates are reported in countries such as Canada, Denmark, Japan, Norway, and Switzerland. Comparisons of the crime rates across multiple nations indicate increases in crime are accompanied by social changes. Crime rates stay relatively stable in traditional societies where people believe that their way of life will continue. Crime rates tend to rise in societies in which there are rapid changes in demographic and economic areas. Crime rates are particularly high in industrial nations that have large cities.[9]

Have you ever heard of the term, "over-zealous prosecutor"? It is inconspicuously surfacing in the justices' systems abroad. Deservedly all the credit goes to the United States as the "model" of how to win convictions with "hits below the belt". It's permeating.

Take the case example of Amanda Knox, a prison guest of the Italian justice system, who was charged with her roommate, Meredith Kercher's

---

[9] Kalish, Carol B., "International Crime Rates" -Bureau of Statistics, May 1988

murder. Kercher was from London and was residing with Knox, while they were both studying in Perugia, Italy. Knox lived in Seattle and attended the University of Washington before studying abroad.

Knox was finally released after an appeals court decision discredited certain DNA evidence and threw out the earlier conviction, which also implicated her boyfriend, Raffaele Sollecito. Italian prosecutor, Giuliano Migini, still insists that the couple is guilty, along with a third person, Rudy Guede, who remains in an Italian prison, serving a 16-year sentence for the crime. Migini's intention is to appeal the decision to Italy's highest criminal court. Most likely for show. In 2016, Knox was on trial for "slandering the police", only to be acquitted because "the crime doesn't exist".

While believed to be all "smoke and mirrors" revealed by the international media, Migini is attempting to cover his own over-zealous attack on both parties, by depicting that Knox, a former high school soccer player, and typical college student, as being some sort of "she-devil". Her involvement was only knowing the victim. This immediately makes you a suspect or person of interest, it doesn't make you a criminal. Even on foreign soil, prosecutors' lust for notoriety through convictions.

Migini's theory, tied to a questionable DNA sample, was that the murder was the result of a sex game gone awry. Yet, the DNA evidence was heavily compromised. The motive was never really established for the brutal stabbing and there were no eye-witnesses. Fortunately, Italy has appeals process that works. Maybe they can share this process with the United States.

Americans seem to compare the Knox case with the Casey Anthony case. Anthony was a partying, hard-hearted, single mother from Florida who was charged with killing her two-year-old daughter. Her acquittal left many people confused and angry. People felt that the prosecution botched up the presentation of the incontestable evidence, just as they did in the OJ Simpson murder case. Neither Simpson nor Anthony was proven guilty and the question will linger forever. Was justice served?

Anthony had been portrayed by the media as a party gal, with a history of emotional and mental issues, and they had convicted her before she even went to court. Of course, this is how she was packaged and processed through the justice system. How would even be possible for her to receive a fair and just trial when many Americans already viewed her as guilty? The twelve individuals that served on the jury in Orange County, Florida, apparently had not paid attention to the media's conviction and delivered a verdict acquitting Anthony.

Comparing Knox with Anthony is almost indiscernible. Knox was a photogenic, personable, and appealing college student, who was railroaded into prison by a sloppy investigation and eager Italian prosecutor. Anthony, on the other hand, was faced by a prosecutor who was unable to convince a jury beyond a reasonable doubt, that she was guilty. You wonder how this is even possible when she failed to report her child as missing for well over a month. This is another example of how inconsistent and erroneous the justice system really is. Which is worse? A system that may actually be letting a killer walk free or one that convicts an innocent person to a lengthy prison sentence that will mess up their lives for a very long time? By placing yourself in Knox's shoes, the obvious lesson cannot be avoided.

Martin Luther King was a catalyst for change. He was self-effacing almost to the point of meekness he said. "Injustice everywhere is a threat to justice everywhere. And, punishment of the innocent makes a mockery of the law".

There are no words that can really describe the pain that wrongful convictions instill in defendants through prosecutorial misconduct. It's a tool used repeatedly by federal prosecutors to secure convictions, nothing more.

John Grisham is an accomplished author of 18 novels. All but one of those novels are fictional. In 2006, he wrote a nonfictional book based on the real-life story of Ronald Keith Williamson.

Williamson was wrongfully convicted in 1998 for a murder that took place in Ada, Oklahoma, where Williamson lived. He was sentenced to die in the electric chair. Five days before his scheduled execution, he was found to be not guilty. His family believed this miracle was an act of God. Finally, we see justice being served.

The prosecutor, in this case, was William Peterson, whose direct and intentional misconduct created a death sentence for Williamson, who spent almost 14 years in prison before his appeal was heard. Serving time on death row looks different than other sentences. It's almost like dead men are walking around, what exactly would they have to look forward to?

During the 14 years Williamson spent on death row, his health deteriorated dramatically and he became a shell of his former self. When you visit an inmate in prison, you get to see what prison walls extract from a man or a woman, along with what they spit back. It's utterly shocking.

Five years after his exoneration in 1999, Williamson was diagnosed with Cirrhosis of the liver and was given a death sentence of six months to live. He died on December 4, 2004. This wrongful conviction robbed him of 14 years of his life, even though he endured and survived, he eventually was robbed again, as he eventually just slipped away.

Grisham took 18 months to research and complete his book which is titled, "**The Innocent Man**". If you have an opportunity to read it, you will see the truth of what takes place. It's an excellent portrayal of just how bad prosecutorial misconduct takes place in our justice system.

William Peterson is an ambitious, over-zealous, apathetic prosecutor. No different from many others. He single-handedly crushed Williamson and his family. It makes you think about the number of others who have been affected by this "administrator of justice" during Peterson's career.

Grisham had this to say, with sarcasm dripping from his voice. "The journey also exposed me to the world of wrongful convictions, something that I, even as a former lawyer, had never spent much time thinking about. This is not a problem peculiar to Oklahoma, far from it. Wrongful convictions occur every month, in every state in this country, and the reasons are all varied and all the same. Bad police work, junk science, faulty eyewitnesses' identifications, bad defense lawyers, lazy and arrogant prosecutors". He continued, "In the cities, the workloads of criminologists are staggering and often give rise to less than professional procedures and conduct. And, in the small towns, the police are often untrained and unchecked. Murders and rapes are still shocking events and people want justice and quickly. They, citizens and jurors, trust their authorities to behave properly. When they don't, the result is Ronald Keith Williamson".[10]

Ronald Keith Williamson was convicted for the murder of Debra Sue Carter in 1988. An inmate came forward and stated that Dennis Fritz was admitting to committing the murder. Fritz was not charged until 5 years

---

[10] Grisham, John, "The Innocent Man", 1982

after Carter's murder due to delays (delayed by state exhumation of the victim after an incorrect analysis of fingerprints at the scene was noted).[11] There were several areas at the crime scene and on the victim's body. Hairs were found and analyzed to "match" both Fritz and Williamson. The semen secretions collected from the victim were indicative of the perpetrators being no secretors, of which both Fritz and Williamson are. There was the bizarre dream that Grisham makes reference to as Williamson is quoted in a police statement which appears to be taken into account in the investigation. Williamson was sentenced to death row.[12]

Williamson's appeals were denied until he petitioned for a writ of habeas corpus. A federal judge granted the petition and ordered a new trial. There were many errors in the initial trial and the DNA evidence did not match. Fritz and Williamson were exonerated and released in April 1999.[13]

<u>Uncle Sam's Magic Carpet</u> is impeccably researched, grippingly told, and filled with 11th-hour drama. The following true stories will terrify anyone who believes in the presumption of innocence and taking personal freedom for granted. It is a read that any concerned American can afford to miss. Studies show that 45% of wrongful convictions are due to prosecutorial misconduct. A large flock of Americans is passively allowing the government to infringe on their liberties in the name of justice. The DOJ and specifically the FBI are using fear as a means to strip the American people of their rights.

Putting an end to this must be a top priority. Something must be done about it. A nation of sheep has bred a government of wolves. Arthur Joseph Goldberg, a former Supreme Court Justice, and Ambassador to the United Nations put it this way. "Law not served by power is an illusion, but power not ruled by law is a menace".[14]

---

[11] https://www.law.umich.edu/special/exoneration/Pages/casedetail.aspx?caseid=3752
[12] https://www.law.umich.edu/special/exoneration/Pages/casedetail.aspx?caseid=3752
[13] https://www.law.umich.edu/special/exoneration/Pages/casedetail.aspx?caseid=3752
[14] Goldberg, Arthur, "The Warren Era of the Supreme Court", 1997

A Deer in the Headlights

Be Realistic

Before you set off on this path ahead of you, make sure that you are realistic with your expectations. Don't overshoot what is feasible for you to obtain while you are doing your time.

A Deer in the Headlights

When you first arrive, you do not know where to turn or what to burn. You take it all in, it's like when you had your first day of kindergarten. It's overwhelming, but don't get too scared. Maybe compare it to your first kiss or the first time you got on a rollercoaster. It's certainly not fun, by any means, and certainly not one that we would want to wish upon anyone.

Not every deer that gets caught in the headlights gets shot, but it's definitely a surprise to them, as it is to you. The expression on your face when you first see a USP camp or prison can be equally as frightening. There it is, high walls with razor wire, electric fences, big towers with men holding guns, we call them sharpshooters with .50 caliber's that can hit you in the backside from a mile away, and of course more razor wire. This is intimidating. You may be coming here only to check in before going to the "camp". It's all unfamiliar territory. Don't look for tents in the "camp", there aren't any.

Once you are processed, you will get a ride to the camp, and your experience has just begun. When you arrive at camp, just walk in the front door, one foot in front of the other. There are no trap doors or some dude who will drop you to the floor and put a golf tee in your mouth to take a shot. You're going to find yourself looking around trying to take it all in. You know that this is going to be home for a while. We all have different sentences and will handle it differently than the next. Your coping skills may be different from mine. Your background, values, morals, and skills are going to be different from the guy you bunk with. It's time to get on board, the ride has begun.

Passing through one building and entering another, this is called Housing Unit B. Welcome to my new home, I thought, shaking my head. You'll be brought into a large room resembling an armory or gymnasium. Everyone is looking around at the other inmates, the ceilings, the metal contraptions, and all of the cubicles. I tell myself that these are my new surroundings, the place where I will eat, drink, sleep, make some friends, and probably create some enemies, this is where I will spend my time.

Nobody throws a rock at me. I get some stares, obviously, they're wondering who the new guy is, what's his name, what's his story, and how long will he be here? They're definitely sizing me up, wondering what kind of guy I am. Don't sweat it, just follow the leader. It's only a matter of time that you will know everyone in here and welcoming a new guy, yourself. In this particular camp, there are around 130 inmates. I have a lot of the same questions that they all have. I pass the showers, the bathrooms, there are some permanent tables and chairs to #10 upper. I get to climb up to my bunk using a three-step ladder. It is here I meet my bunk mate, K.C., who quickly introduces me to the "condo" and reviews with me some of the basic rules. Now you are on your own and you have some information to tuck under your hat. There isn't a lot of small talk, I just give some basic information about myself, then settle in. Ok, I will have to admit, it wasn't like hitting myself with a hammer. I thought to myself that this was doable, I will be able to get through this. You will become aware that the people in the camp are considered non-violent offenders. There are no killers in this camp, whew! A few of the inmates come by to say hello, trying to make me feel comfortable, and this helps. Nobody gives you anything; however, if you seem to be receptive, some of the inmates will tighten you up with a few basic necessities such as shower shoes, a cookie or two, maybe a bible. Some items float around as contraband that another inmate will leave behind. Don't forget, no dead man is clothed when he leaves. When you leave a camp, you certainly don't have the need for a will.

I take a quick tour of my new surrounding and look for a place that I can hide for a while without being too conspicuous, but I am. I can hear the whispers, "who's the new guy?" Don't fret, before you know it, you'll be considered an old timer and people will be coming to you, asking questions. Sleep tight, one day is down and take the rest day by day!

USP-Camp

Here I am, walking into where I'll be spending the next 30 months. Certainly not what I call home, that's for sure. Whatever you do in your life, make sure that you don't do anything that would put you in a USP, whether it is a lower security camp or all the way up to high security.

Over the past several months, I have met just about every CO in the place. I was able to do this due to working in the tool room, along with pumping gas for all of the vehicles on campus. Most of the CO's are pretty nice, at least when they talk with a camper one on one. The others will group everyone together and it is difficult to distinguish who is who. This is a tough pill to swallow. You learn to swallow it and move on, it's just part of the humiliation that you go through at any level.

This particular USP I was sent to was considered high security. All the moves were 10 minute-controlled moves. Each section of the prison is divided by blue, green, red, then further broken down into pads that hold about 100-125 inmates. This is considered dormitory-style, with upper and lower living areas with a common area. Each common area has maybe 4 televisions, a microwave, along with a few tables to sit at. Sure, doesn't seem like much, does it? But for some, this is quite a bit as this is all that they will have as they spend the rest of their lives there. We won't go into what that looks like.

All of these prisons have gangs of all different types. They tend to develop distinct cultures in all facilities. Sure, there are some differences, but for the most part, if you have seen one, you have seen them all. It's at best a meager existence. You would think that someone needs to mentor people about how bad they are and how not to become a participant. However, statistics tell me that in both state and federal prisons, the populations are growing at an alarming rate, and with no clear-cut end in sight.

- *There are 3 million people in jail and prison today, far outpacing population growth and crime. Between 1980 and 2015, the number of people incarcerated increased from roughly 500,000 to 2.2. million.*
- *Despite making up close to 5% of the global population, the U.S. has nearly 25% of the world's prison population.*
- *32% of the US population is represented by African Americans and Hispanics, compared to 56% of the US incarcerated population being represented by African Americans and Hispanics.*
- *In 2014, African Americans constituted 2.3 million, or 34%, of the total 6.8 million correctional population.*
- *African Americans are incarcerated at more than 5 times the rate of whites.*[15]

There is always going to be a replacement for the drug dealer on the street. It is much too lucrative for young people to use this path to their economic advantage. The economy has been inconsistent, which makes it difficult for people to maintain a decent lifestyle. It makes it easy for someone to break the law to supplement their income, generally not seeing the severity of the consequences of their actions. So many people think that they are invincible and with the belief that it won't happen to them. They think they can beat the system. Definitely not the best mindset to have. There is a remarkable underground market in the prison system. You can buy whatever you want through this underground market. From cigarettes to sex. I can't help but to wonder why anyone would take the risks. Is there even a glimpse of what the consequences will be while they are actually thinking about what they're getting ready to do? Why would a good looking, female, CO have sex with 11 different male inmates? Here's what happened: The BOP placed the blame

---

[15] https://naacp.org/resources/criminal-justice-fact-sheet

on the CO, considered it to be rape. She was convicted of rape and sentenced to 25 years in prison.

Not to mention the CO's that smuggle in drugs and cigarettes into the prisons. There was a young guard that brought in some cigarettes one day and before you knew it, it snowballed. He was a husband and father. He wanted to stop his activity, but didn't have the courage to stand up to his answer NO. When they demanded drugs, he brought in drugs, and that's when he realized he was on a path to destruction. He wanted it out, but he was in too deep. He told many inmates that he wanted to die. He chose death. There were a few inmates that gave him instructions. He was told to go to a certain Walmart, at a specific time, buy a specific gun and bring it back with him and that he would meet death, as he wished. Does this sound like a setup or what?

Well, the young guard bought into it. He went to the specific Walmart at a specific time and bought the specific gun he was requested to buy. Guess who was waiting for him when he left the store? The FBI. They arrested him and ended up going to prison. It's hard to believe that he had gotten wrapped up in that mess, but he did. His life now is ruined for selling contraband.

If you can avoid it, don't get involved in this type of activity. It's not worth it at any price of which you will ultimately pay. In the summer of 2012, the market price for a pack of cigarettes, in prison, is $500.00. A carton will go for the same price. It doesn't seem real, does it?

The Compound

I thought I would share the lay out of the compound I was in. I am assuming they're all pretty much the same.

A Glimpse at the Compound

There is the Chapel, with a piano. In between the Chapel and the Resource Center is a barber shop. The Resource Center provides religious materials and educational information. Then there is the A.I.M., which I am clueless as to what's behind those doors. Then you will find the Commissary. The CO sits in the next room behind glass and slides items through a slot. There is an open area outside of the commissary which is used for the dogs to enter. This will also take you to the soccer field, with a quarter-mile track that circles the field. On some days, you will find the same guys walking around the field for hours.

There is a low chain-link fence that encompasses most of the compound. There is no barb wired fences and the chain-link fence could be easily jumped over. Actually, the chain-link fence doesn't even go all the way around the whole grounds. You could easily walk out. There are some guys in here that have made arrangements for drugs, cigarettes, cell phones, and other items to be dropped over the fence. This typically leads to problems, especially if it's alcohol. It's probably a good idea to avoid alcohol at all costs while you are in a camp.

The compound has a very nice sized supply closet that holds sports equipment, exercise paraphernalia, and guitars. The Arts & Crafts room was a decent size and fairly stocked. There are two multipurpose rooms, which where classes are held or movies are shown.

Then there was the gym/recreational room where you found workout equipment (unfortunately no weights), two treadmills, and a Stairmaster. There was a pool table, foosball table, and a TV. Two exercise bikes sat out in the hall. The big poker tournaments are played here.

You won't be able to miss the bathrooms, they're clearly marked. Not too far from them are the administrative offices, the Secretary's office, along with the head CO. Then the CO's office, and the guard room follow. The psychiatrist's office and the health department including the dental office are all grouped together in one area. Then you will find the visiting area, vending machines, and televisions.

The Dining Hall

The dining hall is where you will be served 3 square meals a day. Breakfast is at 6:00 a.m. and at 7:00 a.m. on Saturdays and Sundays. Lunch is at 10:30 a.m. and dinner is at 4:00 p.m. You're not required to attend meals. As a matter of fact, you can sleep as late as you want or work as late as your job will allow.

When a meal is called, it's typically announced over the PA System, the campers will walk in and line up along the railing. Each meal may consist of a protein, such as chicken, beef, pork, fish, or soy. You can always count on a starch such as rice or potatoes. There will most likely be some sort of canned veggie or beans, some form of bread, and usually a salad. You may possibly get a piece of fruit or some sort of a dessert. You will have many options for a drink; ice water, iced tea, lemonade, fruit punch, and coffee are served up here. The CO on duty will announce a last call for the meal and announce when the meal is over. Any meal is referred to as "mainline".

Building:

The building itself is two stories high, with cinderblock walls, cement floors, and exposed steel beams in the ceiling. There aren't two separate floors, it has very high ceilings. Fluorescent lights hang above every bunk. The first three feet of the walls are gray, above that, they are white, along with the ceiling, beams, cables, and light fixtures.

The lay out looks like this. You'll have the bunk area and the bathrooms. The bathrooms can accommodate six urinals and six stalls. There are 12 sinks and a few of them have mirrors. There are 12 shower stalls. You'll appreciate the long hot showers. They're set up with a hook and a little nook for your soap. Another thing you'll appreciate is that those showers are cleaned daily by the orderlies (other inmates).

The television area is one of those rooms that you will find random people in and at random times. Here's a fun fact: if you want to hear the television, you will need a radio. The radios run on a single AAA battery and requires headphones. You can pick up different televisions through them, as well as the many radio stations that will come through.

The laundry room holds four washers and dryers. You'll also find a few microwaves and an ice machine. All of this is complimentary of the USP. Some nights you will find guys in here playing poker.

There is a closet for cleaning supplies and a room or two for the guys that run the dog programs. These are typically campers dedicated to training golden retrievers as seeing eye service dogs. There is one dog in each room. They're very nice and well-behaved.

The CO's office is behind closed doors. You normally don't know what is going on behind those doors.

You have access to six phones 24/7 for 15-minute calls.

There are game tables that seat four players and chessboard and backgammon boards are painted on the top. Campers can also play spades, pinochle and poker at these tables, as well. Other tables seat two and are simply tables and they're located along the windows.

The Bunks:

Each bunk has two beds, two lockers, two chairs, one desk and one shelf. Each bed has one mattress with a pillow built in it. You will need to make another pillow out of extra clothes or pay another camper to sew one for you. How this works is that all transactions are paid by buying the other person things with your commissary funds.

You are given two sheets, two blankets, and anything more is considered contraband. Needless to say, there are a bunch of guys with two mattresses, extra sheets, and extra blankets. Each bunk also has a small trashcan. Each locker has at least one shelf on the inside. You may find more, but it's not likely because some campers ravage up everything that they can when an inmate leaves. There may be a pole to hang clothes but you have to buy the hangers from the commissary. Each locker has a few two-way hooks on the inside and on the outside. The desk and shelf are just two pieces of metal stretched between the lockers. The space between the lockers is wide enough to fit both chairs, side by side. Under the bottom bunk is where you line you shoes and it should contain two hard plastic storage boxes. People keep important papers and/or food in them. The boxes and the lockers can be locked with a combination lock, which can be purchased at the commissary. Many, if not most, campers don't use locks, either because they don't have anything worth locking up or they're trusting.

Additional Must Know(s):

Along with bedding materials, you're issued a number of other necessities. You will receive four pairs of boxers, four white or brown t-shirts, four pair of socks, one pair of boots, one pair of slippers, one pair of gloves, one scarf, and one hat. Your standard uniform is called your "greens". You will receive four pair of green pants, with a button fly, two long-sleeved and two short-sleeved button-up shirts. You will also receive one coat, toothpaste, toothbrush, comb, razors, and two white wash cloths. Comfy sneaker, sandals, and a pair of shower sandals that will cost you extra. You will also get a cloth belt with a plastic buckle.

There are four work assignments. Each camper is expected to work, for which you will be compensated about 12 cents per hour. This goes into your commissary account. The main assignments are landscaping, general maintenance, garage and food services, orderlies, education, and in the rec department. You'll most likely end up in landscaping if you can't demonstrate some sort of skill. That means shoveling snow or cutting grass, depending on the season. Of course, someone is always in charge of keeping the workshop area maintained.

There is also the warehouse, truck drivers, but don't expect to qualify for those positions, as all of the older guys have their hands on them.

Either way, having a view of what the compound is going to look like ahead of time will buffer the shock once you come into the camp. Your mind will fill in the vague or blank spots once you start to get familiarized. Within 90 days, you'll find somewhat of a comfort level, and that feeling of not knowing where you are will dissipate. Everything will blend in with each day, you'll see.

Terminology- Camp

It's always good to learn some of the words and terms that are being used at the camp, just so you have an understanding of what's going on around you. It won't take you long to learn what some of this terminology means.

- A Blast- When the SWAT team rushes a cell to extract someone who doesn't want to leave.
- Bit- Time to serve.
- Down- How much time have you done.
- Book- 20 stamps that are used as a medium of exchange.
- Shank- A knife used to stab someone.
- Burnt Out- Over it, having have served too much time.
- Square- A cigarette.
- Spool- Roll of money.
- Vig- The communion of a bookmaker when a bet is placed.
- Mandate- When a CO is told he has to work.
- Suitcase- When someone hides something in their rectum- the suitcase.
- Mean Mug- When someone looks at you with a mean look, doesn't say much, and is the quiet type.
- On paper- The amount of time you spend on probation after your release.
- Count Time- When you stand by your bunk and get counted.

Check out this dictionary resource for a full listing of terms and their definitions: https://prisonwriters.com/prison-slang/

Under the Radar-Camp

It's not an easy thing to do, but it's important to travel under the radar. This is your ability to avoid all work detail, or will, or any additional argument that a CO may enlist you in. Many have tried, all have failed. It's being able to do nothing to aid or benefit the BOP; being able to do your own thing.

When you first come into the camp, you will have a few days of fidelity, get some sleep and become acquainted with your new surroundings. It won't take long before you may decide to hop on a job that is available. If there is a good job, which are far and few between, you may want to grab that one; otherwise, you may be stuck where you don't want to be. If you don't choose one, then someone may choose one for you. This is usually the camp counselor. There are some hardcore camp counselors that will put everyone to work. The camp in general is a working camp to begin with. It's designed to support the facilities of the USP campus. Some guys come in and it's apparent that they are downright lazy. They were most likely lazy on the outside and probably one of the reasons that led them to camp to begin with. Most likely their attitude follows them around, no matter where they are. These are the guys that make it obvious to everyone that they just do not have a work with or the fortitude to work. On a side note, having a decent job is a benefit. If you can, enjoy it. Since the pay scales are very low in camp, the money can't be the motivator, so enjoy the fact that the job takes you of the camp for 6-8 hours per day. It breaks up the time, and helps pass the day. That works for me!

You wouldn't believe the amount of grumbling you will hear from other inmates about their hours not being correct. Here's something to consider, if you are in a camp or at the USP, you will have to work. The camps are working camps that the exterior of the USP complexes. Basic utility jobs such as yard maintenance or working on the USP vehicles, working in the laundry or the kitchen. You're not going to find a high-level job that requires a master's degree. The pay can vary depending on your skills, knowledge, or experience. Some of the jobs are pretty mindless, they just require a little physical exertion. It amazes me those who don't show up to work have the audacity to complain about their pay.

There area some COs that will take care of their people. Some of them actually appreciate a hard-working camper. Others are by the book, even if you are an outstanding camper and are fabulous with your job. The chances of getting a little extra money are slim to none. It's like they are paying you out of their own pockets or something. Yet, on the flipside, you will find excessive waste, paper in the trash, equipment in the dumpster, and wasted food.

You may meet those who are bitter to begin with. They're in this camp, they've been put here unjustifiably, and will get even by doing nothing. These are what they so call "tough guys". Really? I chuckle when I run across an inmate that look for the easiest job they can get. They do the least they can get by with. In all of the camps, there are the USP or the SFF orderlies. They have AM and PM orderlies that basically clean the bathrooms and the lobby. Each shift they may have 3-4 campers that are working. The more, the merrier. They like to get that type of detail. For instance, 3-4 guys show up at 8:00 a.m. They clean the bathroom, do bare bones cleanup of the visitors holding room and the lobby, and are walking back towards the camp at 9:15. They stick to that solid work ethic, it's their road to recovery. I blame the BOP and the CO's that don't seem to care if something gets done or not. There is no effort to improve a failing system. They end up staying as a part of the problem, never being a part of the solution.

Once you land a *job*, you now have a designation. If not, then you will be classified in a temporary unit. Your name will come up for any and all detail that the CO's may want you to handle. The job attached to a lockdown is one that everyone, besides Steve and I, hates. These guys are the first to go. The CO's can, but rarely do, take someone with a job to a lockdown. They may pick someone who has an orderly to go because they know they're someone that never shows up for work. Lockdown work to most is viewed as punishment.

It's hard to fly under the radar for a long period of time. One camper, Dean, has worked all over the campus, and when he quits one job for another, the COs are pleased. Now, nobody will hire him. Really, how the hell is that you don't qualify for a $1.24 or $1.94/hour job? You have to work pretty hard to earn that distinction. Do anything to be proud of? I don't see it. He is on a temporary unit and flaunts it. Not advisable. Just remember, that what you do on the inside is what you have done and what you will do again on the outside. You should be able to size up some of the others by what they do and how they act while at the camp.

My friend Jeff comes to mind. He's been down for 7 years and a second but is still waiting to go home. He's done with it; he is ready and deserves to go home. He has a wife with a 7-year-old son waiting for him. He doesn't even really know his son. It's a matter of days now before gets a date. He is one of the many that are fallen victims to a poorly administered system left by incompetent and overpaid government workers who don't really care whether he or other inmates have paid their price to society. They have their grasp on them and do not want to let go. I can't help but to wonder why they don't want to send anyone home. Jeff has perfected the art of flying below the radar, finding some peace within himself. There is a way to fly under the radar and he does it best. I want to note that he has a work ethic and is not lazy, he's just over it. This is how his day starts. Shortly after 6:30 a.m., he gets his coffee and reads the paper, which takes about a half hour to read. He then heads over to the rec room where he works out on the treadmill for an hour. Once he's finished there, he will head over to his bunk to wish his buddies a good day. Back at the bunk, where Jeff prepares his gourmet breakfast which consists of a 4-egg omelet filled with the goodies he has left over from the night before. He sits and savors the moment; it's going to be a great day! Around 10:30, Jeff heads towards the beach, or what some dumb pecker beach others call a muscle beach. He has with him a blanket, some lotion, and a read. He's usually content for an hour or two. Occasionally, he gets company, but mainly he's the only one that frequents the beach since beach enthusiast Jimmer left to go home. After a good day at the beach, Jeff will head back to the house for a little workout on the abs, legs, and arms with some buddies. He is feeling great but what is amazing is no CO recognizes that he's missing in action at work. His working the system and is excelling at it. Jeff is working on his mind, body, and soul. He exemplifies what a perfect camper should look like. He's a quiet guy and does not flaunt his ability to fly low. The workout is over, he takes a quick shower before the family returns back from work duty. As 2:30 rolls around, Jeff tries to make the rounds to the working folk, asking how their day was, gathering the details of their day. If you're flying low, you want to make sure that those who fly high and are working hard and are happy to be there. What you don't want is for a camper to be unhappy with his job to a point that could lead attention to you. If you're Dean, who is not well liked, is an obvious target for the CO, you're not in a good spot. You've got to be somebody who can throw back the shots.

Dean's a perfect candidate for becoming a target. He lives in the front near the front door. He sits at a table alone. Whereas, Jeff who lives in the back and quickly exit, if necessary, when a CO is on the prowl. You have to be smart about things, practice situational awareness, and be like Jeff, who has a doctorate in flying low.

Jeff seldom goes to dinner. He has a personal chef that cooks dinner for him around 6:00 pm, it's time to relax. While everyone else is at the dining hall at 4:30 and Jeff's personal chef is preparing his dinner, Jeff who is one of the camps premier chess players will sneak in a game or two. This keeps his mind sharp. You cannot allow your mind to get lazy or weak. If you're about to go home and you really need to have a game plan in place. You do not want to return to a USP camp again. Jeff's there, he's done and he is going home. Jeff wins both chess games, he loves playing Shea or a newbie who thinks he is tough and will beat the pros. Sorry Joe, not today. It's 6:00 p.m., dinner is served. It's nice and quiet and his meal usually consists of a nice steak or piece of chicken. This rounds out the activities of Jeff's day. After dinner Jeff may take on yet another short workout, play chess, go for a walk or visit some of his buddies. Whatever the evening activities are, it's always stress free because there are no COs in the building. Nobody is going to come up to him to do some work. He's home free for yet another day. He once again was able to fly below the radar. Count time hits the floors at 9:00 p.m. and Jeff is always in his bunk. He's relaxed and has a smile on his face. His biggest concern of his day is to get the date that will take him home. Everyone has signed off on him going home or to a halfway house and he's scheduled to go home. Don't forget, the administration tells you nothing. Don't be surprised, if tomorrow's your time to leave…all you need to hear is "Wake Up". Go home, man, go home!

It's been a successful day for Jeff. Another day that he's flown under the radar, built his mind, body, and soul. He's whittled one more day off this time. After count is over, it's the wonderer, a man with a mission, looking for just another moment of some peace and tranquility. Three times a week, he checks his email to see if there is a message from home. Then there is the hopscotch between the two TV rooms for the happiest shows of the season. His thoughts are always in motion, always changing. Sometimes it is a reality show like the Voice or America's Got Talent. Sometimes it's a show like Revenge. Then there are those nights where crazy shows like Sons of Anarchy that area on in the visiting room, of which he will make his way to. Jeff always passes along good cheer to all of whom he meets. It's a different time right now, with nobody in the lead to take his reigns. There are plenty who want it but nobody has risen to the ranks to take over his crown.

David is nowhere as near slick as Jeff and will never be that slick. He's too obvious, too far out there. He is truly trying hard to take over. He has been going to pecker beach, he eats spam in the morning, which is truly a sign of failure. The king of the mountain does not eat span. David is a great guy but lacks in his ability to connect with everyone. There is a chance that with some training he may grow into a better person. What I've learned is that it's difficult to get the stripes off of a zebra. Most likely the type of person you are on the outside will generally carry over to how you will act on the inside. The only difference is that you have certain restrictions on the inside that aren't like on the outside, that you will have to live by. There are a lot of people that don't like David, which means that he could be thrown under the bus. Not everyone can do the impossible for so long like Jeff has. This is an art of itself that takes time, practice, and effort.

You're known, yet unknown during this last lockdown, which lasted 16 days. Because I was the captain of the team, I was able to put a team together, I made sure that Jeff was not ever put on a lockdown crew. If the CO's asked about Jeff, I told them he was busy and could not go. On the other hand, I always made sure that Dave was on the list. Dave did not handle this well and started to pay other inmates to show up in his place. That's definitely not a leader. When I found out who he was paying, I just put them on my list.

Dave needs to earn his stripes, just like Jeff has done. Even when Dave would go up, he really did not do much, and that hurts the team. If you want to succeed you have to play the game. Dave has yet to take the game let alone play it. He's getting there.

For some reason, I've always been concerned about Jeff. Jeff always knows how to rally the troops together when it comes time for a camp work out. He plays softball well. He was on my team the first season and then on the opposing team. He plays shortstop like Jeter, he has a magnet in his glove, and a rocket arm. For some reason, I always hit to him and he never misses and throws me out first. I am slow.

When I pitch to him, he grunts like a mule, and pounds the ball faster and further than anyone. It's the man that can fly below the radar. There may never be another camper like Jeff. Go Home!

I got to know Jeff pretty well while I was camping. He truly exemplifies a true camper. There are some we all want to aspire to be. When I first came to the camp, like everyone else, it takes some time to meet and greet everyone. Slowly you are able to and find some truly interesting people to connect with. Jeff was one of them. I liked Jeff because he is truly a family man. He loves his wife and son. Sure, he's regretted many of his bad decisions and wishes he could live those times so he could change them, but he has to move forward. He leaves in a couple of weeks so he will have that chance.

I was living across from the bathrooms and when I would sit to read and write, my line of vision was right with the urinals. Weird? You bet it was. I had the worst bunk area in the whole camp for about 9 months. The first day I was there, my bunkie got caught with a cell phone, and the CO's tore the bunk area apart looking for more contraband. My bunkie ran out of the dorm and threw the phone into the woods. He was arrested and I never saw him again. Any time I was in my bunk, there was always a scent of urine or feces. It was horrible at first, but take it from me, you learn to stay quiet and live with it. Believe me, as soon as another bunk area opened up, I was on it quickly.

This is how I met everyone at the camp. Jeff was no exception. He would always pick the first urinal which is right in plain sight. It's the shortest urinal which makes it easy for a guy like Jeff who has to lift up the right side of his shorts to take a leak. It's an interesting concept, one that is new to me. Jeff has a small bladder so it was not uncommon to see him at his favorite urinal often. By chance and never by fail, he would look right and there I was. He would laugh at me and I would give him a two-finger eye deal. He knew I was watching everyone to be sure that they washed their hands, heh, well not everyone. It did not take long before Jeff to stop by and pull up a chair to chat. And chat, we did! We never chatted for very long because he always had somewhere to go. To work out or to a scheduled chess game. You see, Jeff made it here at the camp. He had a routine that he followed, one that only he understood. When you get up before dawn to work out and are sitting on your bunk by 7:30 having a drink, sometimes, freshly squeezed orange juice, while waiting for everyone to leave so that you can have your own homemade breakfast, that's a routine. How is it that he was able to make himself an IHop breakfast every morning when the rest of us were suffering with low grade institutional food. The food in prison is what the school systems won't touch or cannot use. It's a step above garbage, that's for sure. Somehow, Jeff was just doing that, no questions asked. Now that I write this, I don't believe I've ever seen Jeff in the dining or chess hall. He was able to eat all his meal without much fanfare.

Jeff is connected with someone for his meals, so he never has to go to the dining room. He has people cooking for him every night. In return, he provides them with his Saturday brunch where he cooks up a henhouse full of eggs and shares them with his people. It works. He lives in Trump on the backend.

Settling In- Camp

If you have a long sentence to serve, then go ahead and buy a good pair of work boots, an MP3 player, or whatever else you need to be more comfortable. Try to organize some shelves so that your items fit in the locker. You will live with a minimal of "things" while you are in here. Let's face it, you've been stripped of everything that you have. Maybe even your dignity, which I hope not. Your space is small, so don't clutter it things that are a waste. You will be given issued clothing, so we all look alike. Hey, your most prized possession may be a fingernail clipper at the end of the day. Maybe a family member will send you pictures to look at and give you hope. Don't forget, you'll eventually go home.

My buddy Jimmer had a less than two years and he decided that his punishment was to buy nothing from the commissary. He would only use what he received from the government, toothpaste and some clothing items. He also took advantage of anything anyone was giving away something for free. Once he took sneakers from the trash. He did not want to ask his family and friends for anything. His punishment was to go without. He had a good job which was a sense of security for him the entire time he was at the camp. He walked out of camp with enough money for the internet and a phone, and maybe an additional $290.00. I think when he first got to the camp, he had a brand-new pair of sneakers and only work them the last few weeks he was at the camp. People would buy honey buns and snacks from the commissary, but not Jimmer. He loved cake day in the chow hall. He would collect people's cake squares and shove them into a drinking glass. He could get at least four of them in there and call it a cupcake! He would enjoy his homemade desserts with some milk after 9:00 p.m. count when he was watching tv. He was a funny guy.

So much for Jimmer, not so much for me. I did not buy any sneakers. I took used ones. I did buy a tv radio and some basic items. It was not my intention to go crazy and buy all these things to make me feel like I was going to be at the camp for life. What I did do, was to organize myself to be comfortable. To have a neat locker, to have my coffee for the morning made up, and I had someone to take care of housekeeping and laundry. It wasn't a bad set up. I kept primarily to myself so I did not put myself out there for criticism. If I decided you were just a trouble maker wearing a mask, I will just not bother with you. Such as the Danny's and the Deans of the world, who are just cutting their own throats. I just walked away. You will find yourself having to make a decision to walk away from those Danny and Deans that you will meet at a USP camp. Fortunately, you will meet just as many good people at the camp and I do mean really good people.

People-Camp

The longer you are at the camp, the more you will question the people who you have lived with. You will get comfortable, say things to so called friends that really are not friends and may find yourself in a tough spot. So, if you were good for six months without issue or incident, continue that course. Don't take a minute and stray with an opinion. It would be best to remain yourself those other campers are not your friends. Sure, there are a group of people that you will like and may even send a Christmas card to. It would be fun to see them later, on the outside, looking in.

Don't make any commitments, it's just not worth it. One guy that I met; Bob has been advising some of the fellows on setting up a trucking company.

He even taught a class. So, thinking that we are right in the middle of an unstable economy, major construction in some areas just isn't taking place. I am not sure I understand how moving dirt can be a viable business. I wonder how many campers today can borrow enough money to buy some dump trucks and start a business. Ok, I get that you may think about things that are reasonable and practical. Maybe, you can really get involved in a business that makes a go of it. There are lots of opportunities, just don't go into business with another camper.

Stay to yourself when you can, be an observer, not in a way that it's noticeable, create a plan, and marvel as to how those people are changing by the day. It sure is stressful from time to time, but its ok time is going by and you will be happy about that. People get to go home each week.

Check this out! I found this letter Dean had written to my kids while we were in the camp together. Thank you, Dean.

"Hello, my name is Dean R. Your father recently shows me a great kindness. The type of kindness one does not expect to find in a place like this. One that must seem in your eyes, insane. If it were any other person that he helped, I may have agreed with you. But the act of kindness was shone upon me. Not only has this solitary act of kindness forever changed how I view humanity, but it has enabled my wife and children the opportunity to have one less burden this holiday season. Which to me is the real gem in the crown that is his act.

I, like your dad, had many real estate holdings at one point in my life. I was not fortunate as your family and lost everything. Including the house my children and wife lived in. I cannot put into words what it feels like to have several years of bad luck culminate in choosing to tell your children that everything they know and understand is about to be taken from them. Nor can I make you understand the hope I now have because for the first time in a while, my wife can breathe. She has one less burden on her shoulders, thanks to a man from Virginia she does not even know.

When we lost our house a few years ago, I was forced to put a great deal of our "life" in storage. As fate would have it, I ended up here, and my wife was not able to maintain the payments. I had adopted the stance in my mind that all was lost and I felt I just had to accept it. Even though all of our children's pictures and mementos from their lives were sure to be lost. I truly felt helpless.

If you are anything like my children, I'm sure you have a great deal of emotion regarding your father's incarceration. If your father is anything like me, I'm sure he has made his share of mistakes. But please don't let a man's short-comings shape and ultimately define who you believe he is. I have known your father for about four months, and in those four months, I can honestly say, I have found a friend for life. I am both proud and honored to have your dad in my life. Not because he loaned me some money. But because his heart has taught this cynical old fool that there still are truly good people on the planet. A concept at age 42, I no longer believed in or aspired to be. I know you guys are younger and don't know what it feels like to float in a boat without any direction in a life full of uncertainty, but honestly, it is a beautiful thing to have a rudder for once.

I hope as the three of you get older and make your ways into this world we live in, that you keep a piece of your father's kindness sticked in the fabric of your soul. Guys like him don't come around too often and the world could use a little more kindness. I hope you feel lucky to have him in your life, I know I do."

Dean R.

Clothing Style-Camp

The clothing style at camp was actually quite comical at times:
- Long johns under shorts, with socks and boots.
- Turned up hats in any way that they will turn.
- Washcloths on the top of your head, seriously!
- Sweatpants with one part of the leg pulled up to mid-calf.
- In the winter, many people want to get overalls mostly so they can either walk or work outside.

I'll never forget meeting Black for the first time, when he came into the camp. He had an overnight bag. I guess he thought he was truly going to Club Med. He had to return the bag to his family and come back through those doors, with only the clothes on his back. What a surprise for him. Black was a great guy…not much of a softball player, but a fun fellow to be around. He adapted pretty well to the environment. You'll see, you tend to hang out with similar folks like yourself. If you are a knuckle head coming in, that's who you will hang out with. If you're a straight arrow, then those are the folks that you will be friendly with.

Bunkie Separation Anxiety- Camp

I was never a big fan of moving from bunk to bunk. I get used to things being the way they are. It's not about being lazy, it's a matter of being comfortable with your bunk mate. You find yourself training that other person and they train you. There are things within our own personalities, our living styles that depend on you clicking with your bunk mate. If you're both slobs, then it's an easy living situation. On the other hand, if you like a neat and tidy living space and your bunk mate is a slob, it can create too much anxiety for both individuals. You also may find yourself with someone who is a bigtime snorer. Both of you will find yourself in need of privacy and some freedom so that you can hold onto some level of reality of what is now your life.

After a period of time, you will become accustomed to your bunk mate. Once you start to get comfortable around that person, everything falls into place. Some guys never want to move because they don't want to have to move their stuff, even though it doesn't take much time to move. If you struggle with your bunk mate, if you do not see eye to eye, or just do not like him, if there is an available bunk, take advantage of the opportunity to move. There are some inmates that will move for position. Someone may have their eye on the penthouse next to all of the windows. Keep your eyes open for opportunities to move if you're not comfortable in your bunk. A few weeks ago, a buddy of mine moved to another area to be near other friends. In that area, they cook every night and have a thing going on. I guess they're what we consider a clique.

Some of the Spanish guys may want to bunk together. People from the same area of the country may choose to bunk together. Sometimes age is a factor when choosing a bunk mate. Keep in mind that if your bunk mate chooses to move, you will have to find another one, or take a chance with the new guy coming in. If you have an opportunity to train him to adapt to your little and insignificant lifestyle, then make it happen. If you know someone who is looking to move and you have a bunk available, then make that perfect arrangement happen. Sometimes things happen, many times, they don't. A long-time resident may want to protect his territory and be sure that they have the right person to live with. We all know that oil doesn't mix well with water, so don't even attempt it.

My bunk mate Tony goes home in a week. I am old enough to be his father. I have gotten to know him fairly well over the past 8.5 months. That seems like a lifetime when you have someone sleeping above you for that long. We actually lived well together. It's been okay. He's going to missed, for sure. I have not gotten a new bunk mate yet, but most likely will have one soon. I live in a pretty good area of the camp, although it's not high end and attractive real estate, it's still pretty good. It's quiet and peaceful, which is good for everyone.

You may experience some separation anxiety if your bunk mate gets sent home or chooses to move. If this happens, you'll quickly realize that this is temporary and once you find a new bunk mate, it will quickly dissipate.

Turnover- Camp

During your time at the camp, you will see many people come and go. The dynamics of the camp will change when this happens. Today, you're considered a newbie, scared, bewildered, and wondering how you will fit in. Of course, you will be faced with a transition period from the day you walk in to the day you start to feel like you belong. Imagine that!! It does not matter if you have 10 years or a year, the initial feeling will all be the same. This is going to be new experience. Everyone will have their own ways to adapt.

You will find people that you can relate with and make some friends. It will make you feel that you are not at a camp, but somewhat like being at a summer boy scout camp. It won't be long before you have a routine and you start to fit in. You will find people that you don't really like and who to stay away from. Within a few weeks, no longer than a month, your routine will be in place and you will learn the ropes of what it's like to be in the camp. Typically, everyone is relatively respectful towards one another. Nobody wants trouble, nor do they want to get into any trouble for any reason. Once you find yourself in trouble to the point where you get a shot. A shot can hurt you in any future effort to get to a halfway house or good time credit to go home.

In our little camp, which is like many of the other camps, if the case managers are doing their job, you will see campers leaving to go to halfway houses or home. Last week, three campers left to go home. When this happens, it gives you a ray of hope. It's great to see them go!

As we have shared, the BOP usually has 20,000 on deck, of those who are ready to come to camp. Some are step down people, others are self-surrenders. It was not but three days when we received a new camper and were told that three more were coming in. It's really kind of cool to have people leave and new people come in. In so much that you now know that your time is getting closer and closer to the end. You have your place when you eat your lunch. You have your job and your routine is in place. Each day is counted for.

As I write this, I've been at the camp for 14 months. It really seems like yesterday when I arrived. I am a veteran for sure. Within the next couple of months, we are going to lose at least 15 more campers. Merry Christmas to those who are up for their releases. Those that get the amount of time in that I have in, will have seen even more turnovers before they are one of them. It may be the reason why some of the long timers just stay to themselves and don't have much to say. They barely even say hello. They just don't want to meet anyone new. At some point you really just get over it, completely and finally over it! The names and faces change but the people are all the same.

One in, one out- it's a revolving door!

People 2- Camp

You cannot help but to get close to a lot of people. It's like your first six month in the military or your freshman year in college. These people will become the only people that you will have day in and day out contact with. They take over your life. As hard as it is to keep a foot out the door in your outside life, you have created a new one, even though only temporarily.

Be careful of what you commit to. Even though most of those that you meet are fine, you don't want to even entertain the thought about creating any business deals with anyone. I know for a fact how many people on the outside really should have taken mine or another's place. Some people are quick to break the law and get away with it. There's no reason to explore the reason behind this, it really doesn't matter. What's important is that you've hopefully accepted a level of responsibility and nobody can say you did not.

One of my friends, Matt, is leaving in a week. I was at the door when he came in with his friend/coworker, Frank. I thought Frank was the one coming here. I was surprised to see that it was Matt, he's a good fellow. He never worked while he was here. He worked out and lost fifty pounds. He had a great vacation. Eight months almost to the day went by like a week. It was totally amazing.

I would be remiss if I did not share Matt's exit. His two buddies, who he played along with on the outside, both spent 6 months at a camp in Michigan. They had a good time eating, drinking, and had a cell phone. It was like they were on a buddy system. Talk about nuts, what a total waste of time. They are picking him up at the bus station. The BOP did not put the paperwork in for Matt to be picked up at the front door. The counselor had it in for him. Sometimes things are just a little crazy. There really is no way to fight it.

Matt's buddies are picking him up on Friday. How cool is that!? They will all go to the Pittsburg airport and fly to Vegas. They have reservations at the Wynn Hotel. Matt plans to play hard for two days and then take the red eye to Virginia Beach to report to his parole officer for a year. He needs to wind down, get a little dose of reality, and some cash. Did I mention a get a haircut, too? I asked him about where he was eating on his trip. He laughed and said "Are you kidding?" "I will be at the Rhino Bar." I asked him how far was it from the hotel, he didn't know. He said, "I've been there a hundred times and I have no idea where it is". Matts going to have some fun, relax, and get some things off of his chest. He'll hang out with his friends for a few days before they go their separate ways. Not a bad way to go home through the backdoor.

Why is Joe here? Someone, please take him away. Maybe you know a Joe? I really did not care for Joe. He had a short sentence, that probably could have been longer. Drugs were his game. He lost a few rounds, smokes like a crack whore on a cold night. He really didn't have much of a personality. He didn't have much to say. He had a persona that he was a tough guy. He had a display of pictures of half-clothed women around his locker. He also owed everyone in the camp money because of his smoking habit. Good luck with collecting that money!

It did not bother me for a long time but then he moved next to me. The guy across from me sold single cigarettes, so Joe would pretend to be his friend and was always there in his bunk looking for a handout, a free smoke. What a leech. Joe is not very smart. I may consider hm illiterate as his speech is lacking. I try to avoid him as much as possible. He had a busy year at the camp. He got divorced and picked up a girlfriend at about the same time. That's tough to do, and really, why bother? You can't make these things up. All you can do is observe and laugh.

Joe has never had anything going for himself and probably never will. You will meet many Joes in your life. As you do, remember to keep walking right past them. They're not worth your time and energy. Associate yourself with someone who has some sort of values or morals.

Whoever said, never trust a con? Never. If you do, you won't be surprised that you may be standing in the park alone and naked. You are totally wasting your time and energy when you associate yourself with similar people like yourself, with similar values, either on the inside or the outside. Some of these guys like to buy stolen property to sell in their convenience stores. If you don't believe me, ask Danny. He was a pawn for his clan and had to do his time.

He made a few friends and had a few enemies. I watched him extort from people at the camp. He had a funny way of making friends, or who he thought were his friends. He would walk around with them and would just hang out. It took him about a year and he was ready to copout on them for eating good. At the last minute, he showed up at their front door like a pauper, begging for food, like a homeless man seeking a handout. Not out of desperation, but just being nice so they would invite him into their club. All I can say is WOW! This one Friday night he is eating with them down at Trump Tower, proud as a peacock, thinking he scored. That's how they are, the Danny's of the world. Always talking, thinking that whatever he is saying means something, when it clearly does not.

He had bought an apple cobbler from the Hispanics. These are always wonderful treats. They're a combination of stewed apples and vanilla wafers served in a bowl you can get in the commissary. While he was enjoying his Friday night meal, his bunkie, Dave, a fun, laid back attorney eats Danny's cobbler. I'm in on it. You go, Dave, eat Danny's cobbler. That is what Danny deserves. You might as well give him the best.

What a great day at camp. You will meet a Danny along the way. Your infiltrators and perpetrators. He is a piece of work. What I can tell you, is when you are in a restricted environment with a group of people, (for most camps it will range from 100-300 people), there is no doubt that they will get on your nerves at some point. You will go in and out of having relationships; some good, and some not. Do not let this stress you out, it's meaningless. It really is. You may stay friends with one or two people, but realistically it makes no sense and a waste of time. You will most likely and hopefully will not ever see these people again.

You will find some of the white collared guys trying to put together another business deal. Some of them will spend hours trying to figure what they are going to do next. That cannot be any good. Did they not learn their lesson the first time around? While you would think so, many don't. Some of their business plans are good, but with no money, usually their families are broken or stretched, you have to wonder how in the world will they start a multi-faceted business. Dean and Dave have put together some strong ideas. Wish them the best of luck and do not steal their ideas and break the law. If you're going to do something, do it right and make a million. The others, those who are into drugs, usually have more of a difficult time when they get out. Some are educated, but most are not. Many people at the camp don't even have a GED and turned to drugs as an easy income source. They just didn't have the skills to get a great job and make it otherwise.

The BOP fails in the area of preventing re-entry. The only way for a camper to prevent re-entry is to have training in a skill set, be honest, treat others fairly and by growing as a person. It's fun to watch these campers hustling anything and everything that they can get their hands on. Disco sells cigarettes to others, some sell new clothes, coolers and other items. There are campers who steal food from the kitchen. You have those who steal from the food warehouse. Someone will make cutters for cutting items, those disappear. The list goes on. It's really unbelievable, but shouldn't be, right? A couple of guys in the camp are dealing drugs. Go ahead, jump right back into business, continue to steal, break the rules, and best of all, try to get one up on the next guy. I have to scratch my head about the future. There may not be one for many of them, potentially for the few who don't mess around and just want to go home.

As you see, there will be all kinds of people doing all kinds of different things to survive. It's a three-ring circus in here.

Who Do You Like? Camp

I know it seems like there is a lot of discussion about people, but for the most part, this is a big aspect while you're in the camp. Let's face it, you're certainly not around anyone else while you're here.

Don't think for a moment that coming to the camp will be like when you met your freshman college roommate, which sometimes turns in to a friend for life. You may end up with a friend for life when you land in a camp, hopefully not. When you really think about it, why would you want to? There are some really nice people that you will meet. People that could have been on your friends list on the outside. There are a lot of people on the outside that break the law every day that could benefit from the camp and the BOP system quite well.

Everyone is different and has a different story. Most of them are pretty good stories and by the time you are ready to go home, you will have heard many stories. This will be perplexing at times. Do you really want to hear everyone's bad luck story? Well, it won't matter, you will hear them anyway. You may even feel sorry for some of the campers once you've heard their story.

Anywhere in the BOP system, what you see may not be what you would get in the long run. People at the camps should be on their best behavior, or you would think they would be. Wouldn't they want to stay out of trouble? They know they can lose their camp status in a heartbeat and to most it's not worth that. The step-down guys have a totally different state of mind and differ from the self-surrender campers. They continue to come across as tough guys, bad asses, all mouth and that's about it. Be prepared, you may be intimidated at times. It's best to avoid any and all relationships with them. You will want to be respectful and cordial when you can do so. Like-minded people tend to stick together and develop a perspective to let it be that way. Do not get involved. There will be enough people at the camp with similar values that you will get along with.

Let me tell you about Jake! He's a stepdown guy. Count on this, you will meet a guy like Jake. When Jake first got to the camp, I helped him out by giving him a few items that he needed. You tend to try to help out the new campers with whatever you can, whether it be by giving them anything extra, like a cup, coffee, radio, or giving them direction on the job opportunities. I introduced Jake to Myers in the landscaping department. I helped him in the tv room and the rules and reputations. Overall, I did what I could to make him feel welcomed which is a nice thing to do. I have a motto, "No harm, no foul".

One Friday night, we are sitting together in the back tv room, watching Shark Tank. Everyone in the room started to get loud. It really got out of control, obnoxious, and downright rude. Because we were basically considered guests in the back tv room, we really couldn't say anything. All you can do is continue to sit there, enjoy the show, and keep your mouth shut. Jake makes a statement about it being loud in there, and I agree, but it's about respect; wrong answer. I should have kept my mouth shut, as it opened the flood gates of attitude. I turned around to face this guy with his horrible attitude and blurted out, "you said what"? I was not talking to him, but to Jake. I just replied, "it's all about respect". This guy that has a terrible attitude is always looking for something to bark about. He wanted to jump into something, and it just so happened to be my comment that he grabbed onto. This is typical of some of the people you will meet.

As I mentioned before, many of them really are not very well educated, they may be street smart, or so they think. There may be thug wannabes. There are guys that are failures on the street, they cannot survive on the street, but when they come into a camp, they are now self-proclaimed bigshots. You will be able to spot them a mile away.

My comment became an issue. Two days later, Jake comes to me and gives me a piece of his mind. For some reason he thinks I have spoken negatively about him in relation to the comment I made. I can't wrap my head around this and want to tell hm to go see a shrink. This is an example of a petty issue you may have to deal with. I told Jake I did not say anything, that he should question the source. What kind of source resides in the walls of the BOP. All you're going to find is drama, idle chatter, and nonsense. He left and that was that. I feel that it was something he started. Perhaps he's a tough guy wannabe with some problems, and wanted to involve me. While the loud noise in the tv room was bothering me, I had a choice, either deal with it or leave. You have to have an understanding as to how to handle yourself while in the camp and make smart decisions. Maybe I should have just ignored Jake when he made the comment about it being loud in the tv room. Being a tough guy wannabe, he didn't have nerve enough to deal with it himself. He wanted me to be his mouthpiece, which by the way, you never want to put yourself in that position. Let the other person handle their own affairs. It's not like it is on the outside, so do yourself a favor and mind your own business. Why bother, it's not going to get you anywhere. Who cares if you have friends or not? You don't need them. Move on.

So that's the story with Jake. I need him like I need another hole in my head. You can cut someone off in a minute, and don't feel bad about it. Jake meant nothing to me. Just remember you don't have to accept anyone's bullshit. Just walk away and ignore them. Remember, you don't have to like everyone. All you have to do is coexist.

You can get by just fine with a few friends, respecting and being considerate to all you come in contact with, but you do not find yourself as subservient to anyone who do not deserve the time of day. I knew I would see Jake again, how could I avoid that, there is only so many places you can go inside the camp.

I took an easy job as a manager of the tool room in the automotive shop which allowed me to write while I was there, and write I did! I almost got cramps in my hand because I wrote so much. I issued the drivers licenses for the USP area and handed out tools, which I had to keep up with. If you checked out a tool from the tool room, it was important that you return it the same day because inventory was done after each shift. Not bad for .10 cents per hour. I felt like I was in heaven.

Myers, one of the landscapers wanted me do his driver's license, which was fine. I did as he asked. I asked Hamm the CO in landscaping to obtain all the information, of which he did. I wasn't going to allow Jake to take any of the tools from the tool room. He was not authorized by a CO and he had to send other campers in to get his tools. One day, he needed gas and didn't know what card to use. Getting gas is a simple procedure, but he didn't have a clue. I was not going to help him and told him so. You should have heard the choice names he called me. I could only hope his bad reaction to NO made him feel better. You go, convict, you go!

The days go on and really, it's not a big deal, none of it is. You don't really want or need to care, it's a waste of your energy. The only thing you want to be concerned about is your own business. Keep it to yourself. I started to hear from others about Jake. You start to compare the Jakes on the inside to the Jakes you know on the outside. There are some Jakes that really work hard to step on other people's toes. The Jakes on the inside who are locked up for a while and don't know how to talk to or deal with other people. What can you do?

You will begin to think, if you did not know any better, that the BOP likes mixing the stepdown guys with the logical self-surrender guys to try to rehabilitate the stepdown guys. They have one foot out the door and most of them need to gain some social skills. So many of these guys are bitter and battered. It's not my job, nor is it yours, to try to help anyone else. Focus on yourself. Don't try to deal with these characters yourself, you're not there to rehabilitate anyone but yourself.

The other night, I am leaving one of the buildings to go to the housing unit. It's polite and respectful to hold the door open for someone when you are in passing. It may be a small thing that you are better off doing, then not. You will find that not everyone does it. I have found plenty of jerks, mainly those who are re-entering the BOP system, will not do so. There are campers that constantly swear because they have an attitude and are just trouble. So, here I am, in between doors, and there is Jake on the outside of the building and he reaches for the door to open it. To hold it open would be a level of respect for me. At that moment, I notice he backs off from reaching for the door and just stands there. He sees me and retracted. Is this a guy you want to stand behind at your friendly Wal-Mart? Think again, no. For a split second, I think to myself, "do I really want to go through and hold the door for him, or turn around and go back into the building"? Either way, I win. Both are giving him the finger. On one hand, it's pleasant, on the other, not so pleasant. It does not matter to me as I am a bigger person and decided that he is totally worthless to me. This is not worth me sweating over. I move forward and push the door open but only for a second. I have no respect for him at all, as a person, as a camper, and not under any circumstances. I, on the other hand, want to be drama free. It may have made him feel good for a moment, but really, my thoughts are good luck to you dude and the horse you rode in on, you're really not worth any of my time and effort.

I share this story merely to stress that you fly under the radar to stay free of any drama. You can associate with who you want to. Just don't expect anyone to go out of their way to help you or vice versa. You can help who you want, but don't expect anything out of it. Remember that the camp is not a place to hold a popularity contest. At the end of the day, nobody really cares about anyone but themselves.

George is another piece of work. Remember, he jumped into a conversation he wasn't invited to participate in. There has never been any reason to help him out. He's another one that I just had to let go of any interaction with. This works for me. As it turns out, fate would have it. He was put on the welding work detail, of which I did payroll for. He came to my office and just stood there. I looked up and he said, "I was told to come to you about my payroll". My reply was, "Really, how interesting"? Interesting how fate works, doesn't it? I took care of his payroll, paying him more than he deserved, to be sure. Ironically, he was told to work the lockdown last week. I had to laugh, guess who organizes the pay for the lockdown, as well? Little ol' me! So, I kept it all up to date and accurate, and submitted the payrolls as I normally do. When everyone got paid, I went to George and asked, "Hey, George, did you get money in your account? Did you get paid?" He looked at me and replied, "Yes, I did" and nothing else. Not even a worthless thank you. So, you see, this type of guy is a waste of your time. You know what goes around eventually comes around in a place like this. As much as you would like to be independent, there are times when it just doesn't happen.

While I am on the subject of losers, I will share with you Dave's story. I like Dave. He's a bible toting lawyer. He's lazy and will most likely laugh at stupid stuff. He says I need the Lord and wants me to attend one of his bible classes that he leads.

It was Thanksgiving, my kids were coming and this was going to be their last visit before I go home. We were sitting next to Dave's family. After the visit, Dave and I are watching tv together and having a few laughs. He pipes up and tells me how close my kids and I are. He can see that we are really connected and sees the love we have for one another. This was a really nice thing for him to say.

He is also friends with his old bunkie, Danny is a piece of work. We were talking about him lying to the others at the camp about me supposedly telling only African Americans not to come into the officer's mess. He created a lot of tension. We have not spoken since lockdown. He's the same Danny that wipes everyone's ass in Trump Tower, so he feels important, and snags a free meal. Those guys at Trump Tower are actually pretty smart. It's amazing they have invited someone like Danny to live in the tower. I guess that they have their reasons, so be it. Their choices are not my business.

Stepping back to the visit, Dave, trying to be cute, tells a story about me running the camp. He frequently referred to me as the mayor. This was going as well as any story from a lawyer could go, until he threw in part that I told these big African American guys that wanted to get some extra French fries that they couldn't come in. What in the world is this guy doing? Dave, you're acting like Danny, lying about things that can hurt someone else. Of course, once he told my kids that story, they knew he was lying. He truly identified himself to my family. Smart people can see right through the nonsense of others. It sure did make him look like a true convict. They looked at me after they heard his comment and asked, "Really"? Are you kidding me? I had told the kids that he was a really nice guy. This really got to me. Seriously Dave, my kids know that I am not a racist, that I would never say anything like that about anyone. Thanks, Dave, what a great impression you gave me, my children, and God. I thought about this situation for a few days and waited for the right opportunity to confront him about his slippery tongue.

Dave was sitting alone in the tv room. I walked in and sat down and said, "Dave, you claim to be a religious man, one who reads and practices the teachings of the Bible". "Yes, I am", he answered proudly. "You know, Dave, I don't think you should ever invite me to another one of your Bible studies you hold again", I continued. He was dumbfounded. He looked at me like a deer in headlights. "Why"? he asked. I quickly and politely recalled the visit with my kids. I said, "Dave, you told my kids that I told big African American guys that they couldn't enter the officer's mess because they were black. I heard it with my own ears, it was an outright and outrageous lie. You had no reason to say it but to be hateful. How do you believe in the word of God and claim to practice it, but turn around and maliciously hurt someone like that with no recourse"? I could see by the look on his face that he did not know how to reply. Trying to lighten it up a little bit, I told him that he knows that it was a lie. Dave knew that Jimmy was in the officer's mess with me the whole day, working side by side with me. I asked him why he would make something like that up and talk about it. He never really could give me a straight answer.

Dave, you go ahead and continue to read the Bible. I have no more time to give to you. He knows where I stand and he knows he got caught. I still have a hard time understanding how he could hurt someone intentionally, laugh about it and then go find peace in a bible. Live your life the right was, as a good Christian. Use the Bible as the cherry on top of the sundae. That's the bonus.

While you're in the camp and you're learning who is who, you'll probably find yourself wondering who to connect with or who to stay away from. You may meet another camper and think that he is an okay guy, maybe the government just singled him out, or maybe he was just another victim. Maybe something similar happened to them that happened to you. Maybe you can say to yourself that you are glad you are here, that you need to be here. I don't know.

You will many of the same type of experiences that I have had. The people will not change much. The stories will be different. You and I, along with the next will have a pretty good story, one that you may take you once or twice around the track. Enjoy it! Share a few laughs, well maybe you shouldn't laugh so hard to those campers who took down victims. Yes, there some guys in here that purposely lied to people to steal their money, and most of the time, all of it. Senior citizens, single parents, and in many cases, their own families. They left their victims devastated and financially ruined. There is no way they will ever get their money back from that person who stole from them, who feels like a victim, and he may be walking with you around the track. You may not run in too many of those type of campers, the Bernie Madoff type, but there a few.

What a place this camp is and it will always be the same. Just remember to take it easy and don't sweat it. It may be some of the best entertainment you will ever get for free. Don't take it personally. Take it one day at a time, but just for a minute to look out for who you may be watching tv with.

Drugs, Alcohol and Gambling-Camp

You may not think that you have a problem with alcohol or drugs, but part of the problem is that you do have one and you don't even recognize it. It's hard to really take a moment and take a good look at yourself. You may be in denial and you are your worst enemy. How is that you got to where you are at to begin with, and most important, how are you going eliminate from your life and keep from even going back there? Is it possible that alcohol, drug use, or gambling created a path to lead you to a USP or camp? This is not an excuse. I've known so many people who have gotten so wrapped up with their dependencies and it's like watching a train derail. There is nothing you can do to stop it, you can try with intervention, but it's not your decision to make. I knew this guy, Johnny, who was a big gambler. He kept losing his money, not only his personal money, but as a CEO of a multi-million-dollar company, he started gambling away their money, as well. He would bet on just about anything, even soccer in third-world countries. He's in camp for three years. He's a transformed man and has his family's support. He claims he is done with gambling, he's ready to go home and is determined that he's not going to ever gamble again.

There are very few programs through the BOP that address gambling; however, they do offer self-help programs for alcohol and drug use. Alcoholics Anonymous and Narcotics Anonymous are just to name a few. There is ARDAP, as well, but this is only for those who qualify with a drug sentence. This program offers some level of rehabilitation. As strict as it is, many inmates take advantage of this program because they will get a year deducted from their sentence.

There is no room in your re-entry process for picking up your bad habits, such as drug and alcohol use. Definitely not worth trying to buy a joint or score some cocaine while you are in a USP or Camp. Unfortunately, poker is a form of entertainment around here. Some people will lose their shirts over a game or two while they're in here. So, keep in mind that it's really in your best interest to stay clear of these things while you are in camp.

Trust-Camp

You probably already know by now, that you really can't trust anyone, especially in the camp. You may think you know someone and everything seems to be just as good as it can be. Then one day, you get blindsided and most likely by someone that you thought you trusted. It's really pretty silly, but it happens.

You may hear everyone's story and why they should not be in this place. Even if they get caught with a smoking gun. Everyone's always innocent, according to them! You know, it was someone else's fault. You'll hear this a lot. As I have said before and will probably tell you again, it's always best that you keep your story to yourself. Everyone is in here for a reason…so be aware and keep quiet.

You will find that in any given year, you may go in and out of different friendships. It's tough to stay with the same people day in and day out, even though some people are just fine to deal with.

There are a number of people who you may think you can trust but you will find you won't be able to. They could be a Bible toting lawyer, preaching the word of God, and pushing you to attend a Bible study.

You may find the guy who you think you can have a decent conversation with only to find out that he's not telling you the full story. Or there is the guy that says one thing today and the opposite tomorrow. Let's face it, you landed at the camp for a reason, most of these guys aren't going to turn off a switch and be the total opposite.

Quite frankly, the only person you can trust is yourself.

The Club-Camp

It's important to remember that when you are entering the camp, that you are not going to a club in the Caribbean, instead, you are serving time in the

Federal BOP system. It's far from a club in the Caribbean. When nice guy Dave came to the camp, he did not show up like he was supposed to. He showed up at the camp with his cool polo yacht club look, carrying a bag full of what he thought he needed, extra clothes, hygiene products, and snacks. You name it, he was bringing it in. Although, I don't think he had a bathing suit, but I know he had just about everything else you would need for a trip to a club in the Caribbean. His sunglasses were the icing on the cake. He must have thought he was going to Club Med.

As soon as walked in, one of the guards quickly told him he was in the wrong place. He had to go to the USP and to leave the bag in the car. He was visibly upset and disappointed that he could not bring in his bag of goodies.

Dave is a lawyer and you may have assumed for a minute that he may have known what a place like this was like and what the expectations would be. He had no clue. He quickly found out that he was not in Club Med. Dave is the only one that I know in the history of the camp to have come in with a bag. Maybe it would have worked if he had a charming personality to pull it off. At least he didn't come in with a tennis racket.

Bad Bunkie-Camp

There are times when there is a bad apple that spoils the crate. You may try to figure out what has created the bad apple, but more importantly you know you have to get rid of that bad apple. There are typically 150 campers on average at the camp. Not everyone is going to get along and that's ok because there are enough people to connect with. You end up with these people and don't mess with the others and vice versa, and it's ok. Don't let it affect you. Don't let it bother you because it's a two-way street.

Sometimes a camper may get stuck with someone that just isn't a good fit, and if that's the case, best that you go your separate ways. It can be a tough spot. It's even worse in the winter when everyone is cooped up. It can be so irritating.

Tony was my bunkie when I first came into the camp. I could tell Tony was raised right. He had manners and an education. We bunked together for the better part of a year and really had a good relationship. He eventually went home and is doing very well.

If you can, pre-arrange for your next bunkie, pick someone that you think you can get along with. You will meet people and get to know them so you should have a feel as to who would be a good bunkmate, and who to stay away from. Be prepared, this process can create some drama and you may be a part of that drama. Here again, don't let it get to you. I can safely say that most things blow over with incident.

When Tony went home, I managed to get Louie as my bunkie, and we were good to go. He was quiet, polite, and respectful. This was a good move and I was pleased. It was a short-term arrangement. He is a smoker and the other smokers talked him into moving down to the rear back door where some of the smokers live. You will find that smokers usually bond and hang out together. It's helpful to have someone to bum a cigarette off of. It's beneficial to them to have an option to sell them or trade them. It's typical for this band of fellows to stay to themselves. They're harmless unless they take your bunkmate and hand you a heroin addict without talking to you first. So, when Louie went to the back and Justin became my third bunkmate. At first, I was okay with it because in the back of my mind I am thinking that I don't have much time and I can live with just about anyone. I don't spend much time in my bunk during the day or night, for that matter. How bad can this be? As I found out it can be pretty bad.

The first thing that I noticed was the 666 number sequence on his locker. This has a satanic, deep dark meaning. He had pictures of crazy things. He told me a judge locked him up immediately for a drug charge since he was a heroin addict. Maybe it was the only way to stop him from using. He told me his detox would take a year. I found out he was a singer in a hardcore rock band. He did not have the talent to play an instrument.

As life went on at the camp, he became friends with a few of the younger guys. He thought they were cool, even if they talked nasty to one another and others. It did not bother any of them that they were offensive. On a side note, I have seen both Justin and his swinging partner. They looked like decent people on the outside but I am sure that they would have been as offended as I was having to put up with their nasty language. It was bad enough listening to how they conversed with one another. It just wasn't cool. Other people were noticing it as well. It's none of my business and I don't want any part of it.

Justin would cut out crazy pictures from magazines and write stupid things on them and post them up. They were mainly slutty, gay, and shocking homosexual things that would make you question his moral compass and his ability to function as a human being in society. Maybe that's why the judge put him in the camp.

I found it best that I mind my own business and that he minds his own business. It was no big deal and I figured I could live through just about anything considering all that I had was 25 weeks left and then I was going home. I let it be and went about my business.

Then on a particular Sunday, out of the blue, he and his ignorant little friend put masking tape on the desk, dividing it in half. They wrote some half-baked, stupid things on the tape. I walked into the bunk area, saw it, and pulled it up and threw it into the trash. His friend made the comment that it didn't last very long. I sat down in my chair and proceeded to finish reading my paper from earlier in the day. I guess it bothered Justin that I made that move. Nice way to find yourself saying and doing the things at the camp that you just wouldn't do at home. As I continued to read my paper, Justin told me to move so that he could make his sandwich and eat. I told him that I was perfectly content where I was and that I wasn't going to move. At that time, his weasel friend decided it was time for him to go.

Justin, in his profound little way, started talking smack, attempting to insult me. He even threatened me by telling me that when he got out, he would find me and fight me. Fight me? Really, where are we in life, middle school. What a brilliant statement he had made. This could be something that you will have to deal with should you end up with a bad bunkie, just another punk or street thug. So, I decided that I wasn't going to move. I didn't budge. I was not going to give him any satisfaction under any circumstances. When he said he wanted to fight, I candidly told him enough is enough and it was time for him to move on out. He had no problem with that. Apparently, he had already been scoping out the neighborhood to move closer to his little friend. They're good for each other, and he serves me no purpose. I expect him to move out.

I mention the incident to a few of the guys at our tv night and two of them mention of some of the stupid things he has done. They both referenced my position and everyone agreed there was something seriously wrong with him. They knew he had been asking around for a new bunk space. As a matter of fact, he wanted to move in with Dave. He even told Dave that he wanted to get that fight over with and was soliciting Dave to join in, so that they could start their relationship. Dave said he was taken aback. He knew that Justin was a punk. So, you see, you just don't know how thing are going to turn out with your bunkie, and how you will really get along.

When John came to the camp, he moved in with Ed, who was handed a 10-year sentence, but is getting out tomorrow. Ed never showers. One night while he was sleeping, Ed shits his pants. He didn't get up to clean up, he just kept sleeping. It stunk to high heaven, what a man! You may end up with someone who is a slob, like Ed. Or you may have a bunkie who is a big-time snorer. This may or may not be an issue for you. Ant farts all the time. It doesn't matter where he is or what time of day, he's always farting. They're terrible and he just laughs about it. There is nothing funny about it, it's disgusting and gross. Hopefully you won't find him as your bunkie.

No matter who you're bunked up with, you will need to learn to talk through the little things that may bother you. It won't be that bad, unless you get a Justin as your bunkie. Just remember to keep a positive attitude and make an attempt to work through any problems you may have with one another. Hopefully you are able to get a good bunkie, and if you do, try to keep him. All will be good.

To be honest, for the most part, everyone at the camp seems to get along with their bunkmate and there is normally a sense of contentment.

You- Camp

I don't like and just maybe I will get lucky, and you won't like me. Yes, we are all different but there is something about you that I just don't like. I can't put my finger on it. Maybe it's the way you dress or talk. Maybe it's the way you treat others. I, myself, like to treat people with respect. Perhaps you don't get that. How hard can this be? Maybe it's something you don't have built in or maybe something you were never taught. You don't have to be a bigshot here. Nobody cares. In the camp, you don't have any more or less than I do, so why do you act like you do? What gives with your attitude? It's like you're trying to hustle something like you did on the street.

Maybe there is an attitude in your walk or how hard you slam the dominoes on the table. Is it really necessary? You're always yelling, especially when it's the time for others to go to bed. Really, I think it's more than that. Is it your laugh that's fake as shit and gets under my skin? Or is it because you don't even have a GED and you act like you're educated. Who do you think you're kidding? It's an entire package that I don't like. Why do you wear one sweat pant leg up, like you're going to wade in a stream? We don't have a stream in the camp.

You can't even spell. I've looked at you trying to type an email out. Can you even put out a full sentence? I watch you sit there and stare at the screen. I know that you're smart because you constantly walk around the camp and remind everyone just how smart you are. You're so cool that I refuse to talk to you. When you say hello, I will give you a pleasant finger gesture but I prefer to save my words for someone else. You won't care because you just won't get it. You think you're the coolest cat in the camp, but you are dirt. I don't care who you are, or what and how you even got here, just stay away from me. You smell bad.

I don't like you and you probably don't like me. It's best that we keep it that way and avoid crossing paths. Forbid me if I ever think we could be friends. I hope you like it here at the camp because you have been tagged as one of those who are coming back. You have the right attitude. You have the right frame of mind to find yourself back in the camp. We won't have to train you, because you've got it down. I am sure glad that people you like are not the same as the ones I like. Your friends act just like you. It gets to the point that I don't want to you and with a little luck, I won't have to.

You will meet people like this in the camp. As I have said, you won't like everyone you meet, and you don't have to. There will be people that may just put you over the top, and you will never have to talk to them. There may be a couple of hundred camper where you're at and may not know them all. Just remember that you are not in a popularity contest. Once again, it doesn't matter in here. Nobody really cares. Just be yourself and hang out with people you like. Have your own routine and be cool. Don't trust the guy that has all of the answers.

There is a lot of joking around so don't be too sensitive to things that are said. You have got to have a thick skin. You may find yourself at the butt end of someone's jokes or criticisms. But cares? Just let it roll of your back. When you first come in, it will be a little tough, but you will. The longer you are in here, the easier it will be to tolerate the people you like and the people you don't like. You will make friends of people that you least expect to be friends with. You may look at yourself and question WHY? How did this even happen? So, it just did and you just go to hell with it. Like water off of a duck's back.

Find that as time goes on, you will be more secure and be able to stand your ground.

Woodpecker-Camp

Can you learn to appreciate the woodpecker as a special bird. The flash of color from its red belly. There is diversity in each woodpecker, in every tree. Just as there is diversity in all of us as individuals seeking our own identity.

Whether it's the people in your life that you identify with, the so-called suits, the hipsters, the bums, or yums, you train your eye well to appreciate the creative distinctiveness of each woodpecker and person you meet.

What makes one woodpecker more special than the other may be the way they sing and make their home. There is a difference between them beyond the traditional rigorous stereotype we may be used to. Watch out for the one that is eager to strike out on his own to be unique but different.

You may want to identify with this woodpecker, the one that is unique and special to you. For that is your woodpecker.

Why Talk-Camp

All you have is time. Your sentence will determine the amount of time you will have to serve. At first, the days will be long until you create a routine and have a schedule. Then you will start to feel comfortable. There won't be a lot of people with a really sketchy background. Chances are high that your best friend or neighbor isn't in the camp with you. It's a new set of people all of whom you don't know. It's really strange at first, but the longer you are there, the easier it will be.

I have been fortunate that I have gotten to know most of the campers here. Today there are 152 or them. They know me, too. There is usually a lot of talking. Most of what everyone is talking about is their sentence, or they want to know about your time in, when you are getting out, or even the system, itself. Some guys even talk about their care. Who knows if you're even getting the truth? Keep that in the back of your mind while you listen and learn to bite your tongue when you have the urge to share your opinion. Your opinion is the useless. You may get away with sharing a story by the campers only care about their families and their cases. It's a lonely place.

It's a slippery slope. Here you are telling your story to someone who has an 8 to 10-year sentence and you're only serving a year. You have to stop and ask yourself why you are insulting someone else when you have it made compared to what the others are having to serve. It's so easy to go through any day and be part of an overheard conversation, and to easily put your two cents in. You may find that sometimes you may say something, and other times, you just watch.

If you're not part of the group, but just on the outside looking in, it's probably best that you just don't say a word. If you're a part of the group, always remember to choose your topic of conversation and your words very carefully. Sometimes I sit with Don at meals. In over the year, he has barely said a word to me. He will answer a question, if asked but that's about it. One day, Tony sat at the table with us. He's a throwback from the 60's, and I found it best to avoid any deep conversations with Tony. Sometimes the depth was limited to "have a good day". It's always best to agree to disagree and leave it that.

Bud was starting to get overly religious and never really comment or answer many questions. Instead, he would answer a question with a question. This was annoying. He is another one that you just don't engage much with.

Sometimes, it's just best to be an observer, keep your mouth shut, and just watch.

Camp Experiences

So now that I have given you an idea of what to expect from the campers, I thought I would share with you some of what the experiences look like. Can it be an easy process? Is it possible that you may even have some fun or decent experiences? Of course, if you have the right frame of mine, anything is possible.

If you don't keep yourself active, have a job, or have an activity, such as working out, it's possible you will start to become depressed and angry. It's important to avoid that as much as possible.

As we discussed, there are a lot of different personalities in the camp. There are just as many different dynamics taking place. You'll be amazed what goes in the BOP system. Remember the focus from the moment you walk in those doors, is on when you are going to go home. So, keep under the radar, mind your own business, be polite and respectful but don't allow yourself to get caught up in someone else's drama.

Kicking Yourself in the Butt

You will want to notice, if you have not already wondered why you put yourself in a position to be a in a camp or worse. There are different people in here and I wanted to take a moment to share with you, what I have observed.

Drug dealers, if you are out there on the streets dealing drugs at a high level and you are smart, know that you risk either state level or Federal level prison time. It's amazing that there some guys who cannot do the math to get their GED, but they can break down a kilo in different weights accurately and quickly. They can also explain their profits. What they also know is the level of risk in getting caught. They may know that the police are looking for them. Whether they catch you red handed or try to link you to a conspiracy, you're always at risk. Let's face it, when they want you, they want you bad enough, it's big enough and just think about all of the money and property the seize in the self-preservation of their job.

You may have friends that have been caught dealing and are serving time. A lot of time, as a matter of fact. It's incredible how heavy those sentences can be for a drug dealer. Think about what that looks like if you've been set up, and it's only a matter of time when you are faced with taking a plea. Don't be surprised should that happen, because it most likely will. Your only option being a 7 to 10 instead of a 20 to 30.

It should be no surprise when the government has you arrested and sentences you to a great deal of time. Once you're in, you're going to meet many people, just like you, but you'll know who may end up back in here again, right away. That's not to say that once a drug dealer, always a drug dealer.

There are many people in the camps that obviously broke the law, but did so by accident. They know there is risk involved, but they're invincible, thinking that they won't get caught. Maybe they've helped someone get a mortgage. Perhaps you budget on a credit card, debit, or a mortgage. The loan is approved, they bought the house, and you broke the law. Yes, you may have helped someone out and the crime is victimless. Nobody got hurt but you're still off to jail. Then there are those who purposely go out and steal from others. Bernie Madoff is one of most hated people in the US. He's doing life for his crimes. Crushing Ponzi schemes. There are campers here who have committed the same type of crimes. John and Pete are two campers that come to mind. They were able to get people to hand over their life savings to invest in an investment company that simply didn't exist. I overheard a conversation that John was having and heard numbers to the tune of 15.2 to 25 million dollars of other people's money found its way into their fake business. This is a huge problem because money victims typically do not recover their losses. It's flabbergasting to hear people in the camp bolstering about their crimes. You never hear any remorse for their victims. It's a tough pill to swallow. You'll eventually see what I mean. If you have any type of a conscious, you'll find those who brag about their crimes to be obnoxious.

Never Say Never

There is always hope if you believe. It's hard sometimes to want to believe when it appears that you are constantly bombarded with negative people and situations or problems. There are always things that happen that are out of our control. Sickness, death, financial challenges, or the loss of a significant other.

You may feel like you are living with a cloud over your head but truly, that may not be the case. They say that the good Lord only gives to people what they can handle. That there is a reason for everything. That your day will come.

Things may have happened and you did not realize it at the time. The truth of the matter is that your time has come and gone and you have really been blessed. You should recognize this and continue to grow.

We sometimes want to give up but we shouldn't and can't do so. There is light at the end of the tunnel and that light is not that far away. You may have to make some decisions and you should and need to work through all of the positives and negatives that you are faced with to achieve the right answers for you. It matters that the answers may affect others in your life.

However, how it affects you is most important. If it doesn't work out, then create a plan B. Just don't never say never.

Time

It's the time you've been sentenced to serve, that matters. You know it has to be done, somehow and someway. You really have no choice. Once you get over the initial shock of where you are, understand the rules, you will hopefully have developed a simple routine and have found some sense of comfort zone. Imagine that, finding a comfort zone within the confines of the BOP system. I would never have guessed that would even be possible, but you'll recognize it when it happens for you. It's certainly not home, by any means.

Whether you are camping for a year or ten years, your goal will be the same. Find your routine, create a schedule, stay busy, and find a purpose.

Work a simple job, make your plans, or if you're even taking the time to help someone out. Do something. Just keep in mind that not much will change from the time you come into the camp until the day you get to go home. Many of the faces will change, but everything else will remain the same. The food is subpar and will remain consistently subpar. The community will only change through what isn't available from one week to the next. Trust me, the beds won't get any softer, man, what's up with that!?

Observe the blank faces everyone sports when they walk in through the front door. They're all taking it in and trying to figure it all out. What's amazing is that stepdown people who know to deal, they have the routine down and are glad to be at the camp. What? You may ask. Why would anyone be glad to be at the camp? It may only take a day for them to fit right in and you may step back and wonder just how they even got into all that trouble, but they do. They tend to make friends really quickly, their stories blend with the old timer's stories, and they quickly find themselves in their comfort zones. There may be a difference and separation between the stepdown guys, long termers, old timers, and the self-surrenders. Those who are in the camp are here just because the government wanted to shock them and justify their endeavors. It's a total shit show and just not right. They have a good time doing so.

Even after time, as the faces change, but the attitudes don't, you may find yourself becoming cynical about life at the camp. Some of the little things that people do when you first arrived are getting under your skin. It gets harder to walk away but you know you should continue to do that. Don't put yourself out there by broadcasting your opinion. It's best to consider that you do not have one. Be prepared, no matter what you say or how you say it, someone is going to take it the wrong way. You probably know someone like this on the outside. Of course, you will probably have someone who will always discredit you and it's not worth it. Stand firm and walk away. You don't have to provide an answer and pretend nobody gives a hoot about anything, because you know they don't. So many times, I have had to walk away from something or someone that I normally wouldn't have.

I used to play a lot of board games like Scrabble and Risk with the same people every day for weeks on end. It was fun for a while, but then I noticed rising tensions within the circle. Some of the participants developed some annoying habits, and I am sure I did too. Whatever those habits may be, they will get on your nerves, and you will find yourself doing whatever you can to avoid them and bail out of any situations that may arise. That's what happened to me with the board game groups, except at some point, I made a point of saying something about being annoyed.

Dean chews ice. He has poor eating behaviors to begin with. Of course, he's one of these people who contend that he's always the best at the game we are playing. It doesn't matter what we are playing, he's the best. Not! We've all tried to thwart his behavior. It was getting so bad that I had to stop playing for a few weeks, this eventually happened monthly. Everyone started coming down on me, making fun of my pettiness, but eventually everyone started to get it. It's not that I didn't want to play any longer, because I did. Dean's bad habits just got the best of me. We were able to remain friends because I created a novel.

Your time in may seem to drag if you're not so luck and are near someone who snores really loudly and badly. It's tough to deal with. It's not like you can get up and move to the guest room so you can get your sleep. No, there is nowhere to go. You have to grit your teeth and bare it. Eventually, you learn to tune it out.

You will also find that at some point, you are going to annoy your bunkie and he will return the favor. I have been with Tony close to 7 months now. He's going home in September. For the most part it's been a good relationship, no big deal. The age difference has been beneficial. We do different things at different times so that we are not always on top of one another all of the time. This creates a workable situation which in itself is good. I will get a new bunkie once Tony leaves. I've been scoping it out. His friend, Graham wants in, so I have agreed. This will take place in three months. I don't mind. I will do the rest of my time with this guy, then I will be done. I think a change now and then is good. It just gives you something to look forward to the next day. I will tell you otherwise, as it can ger really boring. When you're bored, it makes the days, weeks, and months appear to be longer and longer.

Valentine gets to go home today. He was an extraordinary man. He only had three months in and gained 100 pounds. I can't even begin to wonder how that even happened. It's crazy, the food is not that great, how did he do that? You would think coming into camp would be an opportunity to get a hold of your weight, create some sort of exercise program, and get your head on straight. Valentine was loud, sloppy, and not too bright. So long, man.

Just remember that when someone leaves, you're getting a little closer to going home too. Every day that passes is closer to tomorrow.

Bye, Bye

No matter what you have done, right or wrong, guilty or innocent, the judge sentenced you, well it's time to own up to a level of responsibility and prepare yourself for the next phase of your life. Depending on your age, it could be a life sentence. Let's have some hope that is not the case for you and that going home will be sometime down the road.

If you have any decency about you, you will feel disgraced that you have let yourself, your family, friends, and community down. It will probably be the lowest point in your life. Rebuilding that life afterwards is yet another chapter you will need to face. For now, you must get your mind set for what changes are coming your way. You'll need to understand that your life will not be the same. Good, bad, or indifferent.

Hopefully, you have come to the realization that you may have some troubles ahead. Many of us have no idea what to expect, so we are going into this like the blind man leading the blind. If you have been sitting in the county jail, what we can say for sure is that life is about to get better. Maybe not a lot better, but better. If you're in the county jail, you will see it all. When you get to your destination, hopefully a camp, you will hear countless stories about the cruelty that takes place in the county jails. I've never heard otherwise.

Upon your arrival, whether it be at a county jail or a self-surrender into a camp, you must be able to make the transition to your new life. If you do not do it yourself, the situation will break you down, it will force you to change, and you change you definitely will. Just do whatever you can do to keep your wits about you. You will meet a circus of people, all kinds that have committed just about every crime imaginable. Of course, they are all innocent. You will not be the person you were on the outside. On the inside, you are just a last name and a number. The power you thought you once had, is completely stripped away. Everyone is equal in here.

Be aware of the bad actors, the tough guy wannabes, and yes, the tough guys who may intimidate you and like bad guys, but they're acting too.

Don't be in a rush. Don't overthink a situation. Try to wrap your arms around the time that you have to do. Get settled in and the days will start clicking away, and before you know it, you will be close to getting out. It's always one day at a time. Don't go to a camp thinking that you are innocent and you have been wrongly sentenced. Whatever you did, you got caught. You pleaded your case or you went through a trial. You may think this is a free country and there is a justice system. There are a lot of flaws including those overzealous prosecutors and far-reaching federal sentencing guidelines that put people away for way too long. It's what people tend to get when they've committed a crime.

Don't be a pathetic and cowardly victim, stand tall, and take your medicine. Sorry, but you meet a lot of people who did nothing, and the government made them their victim. The government may be out to get you for some reason. They can find fault with everyone and you may be surprised that even you can end up in a federal prison. Stay below the radar as much as you can. Do not put yourself out there. Don't hang onto the theory that you were singled out, that you were wronged, man. You will have to knock that chip off of your shoulder, otherwise, someone else will do it for you. I don't think you want that to happen. If there are victims to your crimes, they will most likely want and expect you to have a long-term sentence, maybe even life. If you go in feeling like a victim, yourself, it will make time crawl by very slowly.

Everyone at the camp my feel like a victim and that they don't belong there. If you can, avoid sharing your story with so many fellow campers. They all have a similar story, they all claim to be innocent, and really don't care to hear about yours. Find a level of humility, it will make your life easier. It usually comes at the darkest hour of your life and from there you can start building your future. You will not have employees, power, money, or family. You won't be able to buy your way out of a jam. You will be like all of the folks you now live with and you're all equal. You should try to be either humbled or genuinely remorseful for what you have done to put you here. Remain free from any level of denial. If you don't, in time you will be forced to. You may find someone who is weak or eager to lend you an ear. Maybe they will listen to your story. It's tough to take the bully out, or to take on a con man. I have seen many con men prey on the weaker camper, who threw out a lifetime looking for some level of salvation. They are in here, so be aware of them. This is surely not a good way to go.

There is a camper who was once powerful on the outside. His new job is in the kitchen, washing pots and pans. He hates it. Some people love it, but it's not for him. The kitchen was once controlled by an inmate named Joe. He even had his own office. Joe ran the black market where he sold extra meals and veggies. He was in charge. It did not take him long to figure out what he has to do to get out of the kitchen. He hustled a carton of cigarettes and one day while he was in his office, he slipped the other inmate the carton. In good favor, he asked the new inmate if he would like a promotion to handling the silverware. The inmate jumped on the new job, he got out of pots and pans.

You'll have to figure out your own gig. Whose bun to butter. There are some buns to butter. Just lay low. Take one day at a time. Keep your expectation levels to a minimum. That you won't be disappointed if nothing comes your way. You won't find any trouble that way.

Keep busy and keep your nose clean!

Oranges

If you're thinking for any reason that you want to hit someone or beat them up, I would not recommend it. Some people will put a bag of oranges together and beat someone with it. It's a crazy concept, but it will not bruise the person on the outside, only on the inside. You can do some serious damage by beating someone. Can you believe the extent some people go to?

First things first, do not ever be tempted to hurt, hit, or touch anyone, at any time. No questions asked, who did what, who's at fault, the guilt is shared and both parties will have to say so long. Think before you do whatever you're going to do. Think before you say anything. My advice is to lay low, keep your thoughts and opinions to yourself, it makes no difference to anyone, but yourself. You will one of many, all the same.

Just Too Cool

Are you just that tough and so cool that you have no remorse for why you are at the camp? You must have done something to get you here, right? It's nice to know that you are getting ready to go home soon, and that's pretty cool. You know things will be different. What was then, is not now. If you're planning on hiding anything, it won't be the case today. Anyone with the internet can access Google and find out everything and anything about you. Someone you don't know, someone you've just met, a prospective employer, or even a debt collector can find your profile online. Don't be surprised if you face rejection over and over again. Look at where you have been, it's better than where you are now. You are free to do what you pretty much want to do, pursue your adventures, and maybe grow a little. It's all good.

Maybe you're just not that cool anymore. You are who you are, someone who has faced his mistakes, admitted his guilt, and paid the price to society, so it's time to move on. There are times that society does not want to move on, so you must work the odds that may be stacked against you. Put them in your favor, make them work for you. Don't think that the world will welcome you home with open arms and that you will feel rejoiced. Do what you can to keep yourself strong so that you can fly high. You will have healing to do and so will your loved ones. Most will just look at you as a bad guy and a criminal. They may even think you should have been in for even longer than you were. Don't care what others think of you. Overcome the objections by not going to the pity party. Go to the land of success. You can do it.

You may find yourself on the defense. Try not to. You've paid your dues. You are now a new man with new challenges that are on the horizon. Sure enough, there are going to be those people who will throw a pity party for you. They will continue to dampen your spirits. While it is easier said than done, try to ignore this, especially from loved ones. My ex-wife has been unhappy for a very long time. When my mother was alone, they fed off of one another. It was especially nice to be invited to dinner in an effort to chastise me. This worked especially well for them in front of other people, including my children. You want to defend yourself or say something in response, and while many times I did, it fell on deaf ears, like a slue slayer to a dragon. I would especially like it when they made corn on the cob and would they make plenty of it. I would eat a piece, some of the other guests would eat their share, while others would not. Once everyone was done, I would help myself to a second or third piece. Keep in mind that these were regular sized ears that my mother broke in half in order to fit them all in the pot. That's all they needed. Yet I would hear, "Why are you eating all of the corn?" "Are you going to leave some for anyone else?" "I'm sure glad I made enough". These just a few of the comments they would blurt out. Talk about making someone feel like shit, they sure did a great job of it. They very seldom paid me any complements. I never heard, "Did you have a nice day?" or "I like that shirt on you". My mother passed away two years ago and I won't miss her unhappy, sarcastic self. I only have to deal with Margaret, my ex-wife, who is particularly good at being able to give me double whammy, since my mother is no longer alive. She enjoys it. For a hot minute, I thought maybe this would change as we sit down for a nice holiday meal. I suspect that there are many miracles that the Good Lord has blessed people with, and I am sure that one of them would not be that Margaret would ever say anything nice to me. She has a way of saving all of those nice remarks for other people. Do you think that there will be a flag waving, corn eating party when I get home? I am 100% sure the answer to that is NO. You may have a Margaret in your life, but then again, maybe you don't. For your sake, I hope not.

What's extremely difficult to live with at times, is the rejection, the disappointment, and embarrassment that you will face, whether you deserve it or not. What I love about my observation of Margaret, is that she pretends to be a good Catholic girl. She goes to church regularly and even teaches Sunday school to little children. I think it's truly wonderful that she does this, but how many people can go to church but then turn around and be cruel to others? I don't think some people even have a clue. Don't they know that God is watching them daily, not just on Sunday?

Maybe you have a Margaret in your life, I'm almost positive you do, and I bet you will get a ton of abuse and ridicule, as I have shared in this story. Be a pillar of strength and wisdom. Don't let your guard down and when the Margaret you know takes aim, do the best that you can to understand her. Understand that in the end, they will be facing God. Avoid altercations with the Margaret's you will meet. Stand tall, be strong, and take the rejection as a blessing. If anything, it will make you see what you don't want to be like.

I have this fantasy that judgment day comes and the gates to heaven open. Wouldn't it be something to wonder about, if you were easily brought in, and your Margaret was not?

3 Hots and a Cot

It's not so bad. You will work the processes in your mind over a hundred plus times, and may never really imagine what it's like. If you're a stepdown guy, you know the deal, and time in a camp is surely a piece of cake. Please check your attitude in at the door. Most don't and come to a camp like they own it. They are the toughest to deal with. A simple hello is tough to get out of them. If you are curious about what it's like at the top, then you can get your fill of information from them. Some of that information, the stories, are exaggeration in that you know that you're not there and are in your comfortable little spot, 3 hots and a cot.

You won't have to worry about the 10-minute moves, the gangs, and the locked cages they live in, so when a stepdown guy comes into a camp, it's almost a sense of freedom for them. Good for them, they deserve it and have earned it. Many will have that prison thug mentality. Tough people to deal with and you may find some peace with the self-surrender.

There are some good stepdown guys who truly respect the fact they are in camp, and will go out of their way for everyone. There are peacemakers, who build the wall between the stepdown guys and the self-surrenders. I do mean that figuratively, an actual physical wall hasn't been built. There is this stepdown guy by the name of Rudy, who has stood up for many campers over all kinds of issues such as television, food, living arrangements, etc. When it's right, it's right and needs to be for everyone involved. So, Rudy is a good, solid guy. You will meet people like Rudy. Rudy has paid his dues, he is ready to go home, and really should go home.

The self-surrender guys take a little more time to adjust, and adjust you will. Some long than others, depending on how long it takes you to adapt. It's not that difficult.

Realistically, if you have over 5 years to do anywhere, be sure you are ready to settle in. It's difficult enough to adjust to your new environment, but to think about 5 years, 8 years, or even 10 years for some people my age, it's going to be a lifetime. It's not necessarily the death sentence but it feels like it. Nobody wants to ever think that. It would be nice if the politicians realize that too much time has been given out over the years and that the cost of this is tremendous. It's a crime in itself based on the amount of time that is being handed out, when will someone get that? Maybe there is another school of thought for repeat offenders, I get that.

Let's hope that at some point there is a change in the system and people can get some relief, they need relief. Not to mention, that instead of building more prisons, we should work on stopping the people being sentenced and incarcerated. This would be a great start.

There ae many people that I have met that are really having a hard time, trying to desperately get their hands wrapped around a big old oak tree. I don't know how some of them are even doing it. Alberto, a nice guy that I check tools out for, lives next to my bunk area. He came in with 10 years. He has a wife and three kids, and 10 years. He has a better attitude towards prison than I would have. He talked about a 2255 all of the time. All I could do was wish him the best of luck. They need to have just given him a few years and then send him home.

You will meet many nice guys like Alberto. Your new circle of friends and acquaintances, day in and day out are talking about the same things, day in, and day out. Nobody cares who you are or what your story is. They are engrossed with their own problems. All you can do really, is just listen, offer what advice you may want to give, be a friend, don't criticize, and you should be okay. It's always a good idea to allow them to run the conversation. There are some that think, well, they are convinced, that they are always right. We all know those people, don't we? Do yourself a favor, let them think that they're right.

In the meantime, enjoy your 3 hots (hot meals) and a cot. Things could be much worse. Be grateful for what it is or what it could have been.

Religion

I have not been to too many masses here at the camp. The BOP in general honors your choice of religion and will go out of their way to make sure that your rituals, holidays, and beliefs are respected. They do a pretty decent job of accommodating these privileges to the point where it could be taken advantage of.

Hopefully, you will be able to pick up on who is real and who is not. Just by watching others pick up their bibles, or having found a new path, or maybe those who have just found Christ, is plenty of indication of who is serious about their religion. They just go with it. It's too bad they did not find it prior to getting into trouble, maybe it would have saved everyone a lot of time and money.

There are a lot of Muslims and the BOP honors all of their holidays. Right now, we are in the middle of Ramadan. They fast, eating only prior to sunrise and at sunset. There is no consumption of food or drink during the day. There are a quite a few in the camp that I am at. It's quite surprising as there are more than I would have thought. My friend, Steve, who lost half is body weight is a white, blue-eyed, blonde Muslim. He loves it because he can have many wives, and indeed, he does. You go, Steve! This could a good thing in life, having many wives. During Ramadan, at the pen, there are actually 500 Muslims out of 1600 inmates. Instead of boxed lunches, they provide private seating at the mess hall, so they can all dine together. That's awfully nice of them. This is not necessarily such a good situation for the CO's. This becomes a great excuse for all of the Muslims from different pads to talk, pass notes, and plan their next move. Everyone knows what they're up to, and it's not good. They don't want all of this planning going on, so the Ramadan meal is more than just a meal, it's a vehicle for communication.

It's a Sunday in 2012, the Catholic priest who provided a mass that I attended at USP told this story today. He was about to hold mass at the pen and 156 inmates showed up, again from all different parts of the pen. It was a way for all of these inmates to communicate, at the expense of hearing and learning the word of God. The priest saw what was going on and canceled the mass. Had the guards escort them all to their pads, mass wouldn't have gotten canceled.

What a waste of time. I guess the priest thought this was a great story, so he decided to share it at the camp mass. It can't get any shallower than that.

Pick your poison. Pursue your religious beliefs, whatever they are, as best as you possibly can. Practice them because you believe from your heart and soul to learn the teachings of your religious beliefs.

I would be remiss if I did not tell you about Danny, who exceeds all limits of human kindness. He carries a Bible, wears a cross around his neck and arm, but seems to be taken over by the anti-Christ. His life is full of demons and watching him pray gives you a sense of peace, because you're hoping his demons will be cast away. I can't but to hope that he will receive peace somewhere in his life, which today, is full of lies, cheating, stealing, and demoralizing the human spirit. His demons are clearly taking over his soul. After only being at the camp for 8 months, he has fallen back into his old habits. He's gambling any chance he possibly can, every night after mess, you will find him at it. He owes most of those he gambles with at the camp a lot of money. You don't want to owe anyone in the camp or the pen any money. Not even a penny. You want to avoid temptation at all cost. You may find yourself in a tough spot that you cannot get out of and will probably be forced into doing things that you know are wrong.

This is a crazy story. I couldn't believe it when I heard it. A family of one of the inmates came to visit last weekend. The inmate's wife and her two children were here. Through the phone, email, and mail, the CO's had reason to believe that she was going to smuggle some heroin into the visiting room. She would pass it to him so he could bring it into the pen. Keep in mind that there are more drugs inside a BOP facility than you can even imagine. It's unreal and the value of it all would knock your socks off. Why would she do this?

Apparently, she hid the drugs in her private parts and sometime during the visit, she used the ladies' restroom, and removed the drugs. The COs were on top of it. There was a female guard in the visiting room and gave her sometime in the rest room, then proceeded to go in to recover the drugs, Unfortunately, this inmate's wife and mother of two, was arrested immediately. Child protective services were called and their children were taken into their care. I can't even imagine why she would even risk that. The kids will now be a part of the system, unless there is an available family member to take them in. The woman will be charged and looking at serving 5 to 10 years in a federal prison. It's easy to overthink situations like this, but we do know there is so much pressure in a USP that this poor inmate could have done it for a few reasons. Maybe he owed someone for something and this was the way he was going to pay that person back. It could have been a do or die situation. Maybe it was the pressure that made him involve his wife on the outside. Maybe it's a matter of money and greed. The one who controls the money, the drugs, is the one who is in control. When you have control, you have power.

This inmate has nothing to lose for heaven's sake. Why in the world would they put themselves at risk, or better yet, put their family in a situation that they could and in this case go to jail for, for a very long time. This family had a chance, but it was lost because of sheer stupidity. I mean, what's wrong with her? Hadn't she thought about the fact that her husband was already in prison? Is there no understanding between right and wrong? I have seen this first hand as I am living the nightmare. Don't put your people in a position where they could fail and fall hard. If I were to ask you to follow me then jump off of a bridge, would you? Maybe you should not jump.

We continue to work hard to find our own peace. We all have a different way to achieve those goals. There is a platform for all of us. You should not be someone that you are not. Be yourself but most importantly, be true to yourself, don't be someone you are not. Don't hide behind your Bible or your religion. Learn to live your life everyday as a Christian, knowing the difference between right and wrong. Practice this.

Take the right path towards peace and freedom for yourself. Instead of putting people in harm's way or hurting others, take a minute and help someone. For all those that you help, there will be a reward at some point. Sometime when you least expect it.

When you have accomplished this effort in your life inside, you can honestly say that you are on your way home.

Family- Camp

It was Father's Day in 2012 and I did not have a visit from my children. I did not get a card or a call either this particular Father's Day. If I were a drinking man, I would be a drunk. If I were a drug addict, I would go off the deep end. You can't talk about family and leave one spoke of the wheel out. Many will say that it's ok. It's not ok, it just doesn't work that way. Whether or not times are good or bad, family needs to and should stay together, especially when times are tough and a family member needs to stay together. Where are you and what are you going to do to keep your family together?

How many times can you break my heart? Especially when there is nothing left to break. At some point, you would think that they would get it, or maybe they never will. Selfish people continue to be selfish and do not have the ability to be compassionate. They just won't achieve their right and their love to do so. It's a shame and quite frankly, I hate it for them.

My three grown kids and not one of them acknowledged me on this particular Father's Day. There is a scar that will be there for a very long time, and I hate that. What a loss. Another chapter out of my brother's book on how to destroy a family on a dollar.

Volunteer-Camp

If you want, you can volunteer while you're in camp. I haven't seen too many people volunteer for anything. There are no brownie points in a place like this. Nobody really cares about anything or anyone, ever. A CO may show a little appreciation if you help him/her out with something. Most of the time, it will be presented in the form of an order, so you're really not volunteering to help. Don't expect anything back in return because most of the time you will get nothing. If you help someone out, great, then move on. Whatever you do, do not hang onto it. You're certainly not going to get any extra money out of volunteering. You won't get out early. You won't that extra piece of chicken or a few more fries. You get nothing.

You're actually expected to do what they, the CO's, want you to do. You can refuse, but all that is going to do is to land you with a shot, and trouble. It's like the old saying goes, "You're damned if you do, and damned if you don't". I would say most people don't. They go about their business and mind their own business, just lay low and stay below the radar, it's the only way to get through your days and nights.

Pill Line-Camp

This is almost hysterical. Three or four times a day, a nurse will call the pill line. That's when you are called in because you're on medication. In order to take that medication, you will go to a nurse's station so they can dispense it for you. The USP has medical facilities and those specific facilities will provide you with greater care. The inmates love the pill line. There a couple of nurses who put all of the pills on a cart and go from unit to unit to dispense the pills. It takes a lot of time and you will see many inmates waiting all day for their pill call. I shake my head in amazement. One time, I asked someone why there is a pill line instead of a dispensary. I was told that there are too many irresponsible people and it would never work. Some may overdose, others would sell their medications, and some may not take them as directed. You get all kinds in here.

Getting your pills for some is like a child at Christmas. You get these nice little bags with the medication in them. Some inmates get a lot of little bags. One guy has a walker with a compartment in it that acts like a seat, so that he can roll and stroll. He keeps toilet paper, his medications, and cookies in there. You wouldn't imagine just how much medication costs the BOP each year. I don't know the exact figure, but it's got to be a lot, just about everyone stands in line for something.

Stages-Camp

You will change a little while you're at the camp. The change will depend solely on you. At one point, I got close to Dean. It went from good to bad, and even worse. He lowered his standards and became a camp hood. Today he asked me why nobody wanted to hire him for a work detail. He wanted to know what it was that people did not like about him. Well, maybe that's what he needs to work on over the next few years, as he plows through his time.

You want to stay focused on getting out, but do not become obsessed. Stay true to who you are. Don't get involved with anyone with some type of business scheme. One, it's not approved and second, why bother? Stay focused on what you did on the outside, something that made you happy, your family and friends, business people, or anything or anyone that will keep your mind occupied with everything but the nonsense of the camp. There is a lot nonsense.

Everyone does their time differently. Most inmates work. Many work out, play cards, watch tv, sleep, or read books. What will be your remedy? In the beginning, I played cards and boardgames, but quickly got bored. It also puts you in a tough spot because you have to deal with different personalities. Yep, you've guessed it, there are still cheats, sore losers, and egos that you need to put up with. After a while, you find yourself not interested, so you move onto something else.

You may find different people to work and associate with. As they come and go, so will your interests. Some guys will change jobs a few times. Not me. I was content to stay in the same bunk area, although I did change once. I had kept the same job, as a matter of fact, when I wanted to switch jobs, the boss man, who is a real strict managerial type, said NO, I could not switch jobs. Well, thanks a lot, fellow.

Your time will move on a day is long, a weekend is longer, but a month goes by quickly. Just make sure that you pull on a line when the bobber goes down,

Don't Drive Your Car Down a One-way Street- Camp, Inspiration

Pay attention to what you're doing. Don't cross the line. Be observant of what is around you. Don't let life play tricks on you. You're smart and there is no reason to take the wrong turn to go down any one-way street. There are plenty of signs to warn you. You just have to want to see them and adhere to them. Nobody can do it for you. You have to do it for yourself. Keep moving in the right direction.

Crazy Days-Camp

The other day, when our campers were working at the USP commissary, an inmate comes up to the window to retrieve his commissary, and the CO tells him no, that he wasn't getting his commissary on that particular day. The inmate retaliates by taking out his penis and urinates in the shoot that is used as a pass-through for items you want to buy. He then tells the CO, "I guess nobody will be getting their commissary today", and walks away. It's pretty bad at a USP, and you do not ever want to go there. It's a vicious place to land in.

I went next door to the welding shop today just to check out what everyone was doing. I ran into Freddy, my buddy from Kentucky, who was working on a large, flat piece of metal with holes in it. He tells me that he's making a bed. Cool, I think to myself, but question why, it's no different. Although this bed was a little bigger than the normal bunks, it had horseshoe straps on each side, for of them. There were eight total. Then I realized it was a restraint bed for when an inmate is restrained to a bed, as well were on the flat part were pee holes. This was for the inmate to urinate without having to be released from the bed, the pee will flow to the floor. Holy crap! This is as bad as it gets. Can you imagine how rough it is?

Last week, Freddy was to make a cage about the size of a small desk. It was going to accommodate a chair, which was not very big or comfortable. What they wanted was a cage for holding an unruly inmate. They would handcuff the inmate to this cage. The cage was to be put in the Lieutenant's office. If there was an inmate at the USP that got into trouble, he would need to report to the Lieutenant, then would have to sit in that chair that was in the cage. It reminds me from a scene out of Hannibal Lector. This is really, really crazy.

Old Hat- Camp

Nothing is going to change much while you are doing your time. The conversations will get stale. It's always nice to talk to someone who keeps up with the daily news. Out of the 154 people today, I think maybe only 8 watch the news. I would say there really isn't not much to talk about to the rest of those at the camp. They don't have a clue as to what's going on outside of the camp. It's ok. They may know more about sports than you do, or the music jams on BET, but they can't tell you the two VP candidates are that are running during the 2012 Presidential election.

You will have to find something to do to pass your time. Find that routine and stick with it. Time will fly by, if you do. I can promise you that. Don't expect much to happen. It's usually pretty boring around here. You'll find that one day will run into another and another. Unless you are reading a daily paper or two, checking the news, catching up on emails or getting letters, you can expect to quickly get and stay out of touch with the outside. You find yourself living your daily routine. You either bitch about the food, or love it. It's always interesting to check out the incoming campers. Sometimes you may find yourself hunting down a green pepper. The things that usually took little thought on the outside become big efforts on the inside. I've attempted to open conversations with others about who they were interested in for the upcoming Presidential race, many did not even know who was running, some didn't care, and only a few knew about any of the issues being addressed.

Many campers will keep up with their children or families and spend hours upon hours on the phone talking with them This is a positive step in the right direction for many of them and enables them to keep in touch and connected to the outside world.

When you finally get out, there is a re-adjustment time, which may be a few weeks for some, may be a few months for others. It really depends on the individual and what they have going on for themselves. It may be the ability to get a job, to find a place to live, or just to be able to spring back into action. Everyone will have their own threshold to measure how long it will take.

The longer you are at the camp, the more settled you will become. You get accustomed to the small metal beds, the food, the rec times, the lousy job and pay. You may connect and make a few friends, and this is all pretty good. Some people you will keep up with after you get out, others you won't. Everyone is different.

Being able to get your local newspaper is great because it keeps you connected to what's going on in your hometown. I have been looking at the obituaries, only because I want to see who I have lost while I've been in here. I am not morbid. I just don't want any surprises when I get out. You will realize that life on the outside moves on whether you are there or not. You'll realize that the older you get that the time flies by faster and faster.

So, as you can see, it's really important to keep yourself busy. Keep yourself connected to the outside, if you can. Soon you'll find yourself on the outside looking in.

Winter- Camp

Winter is difficult in the camp. After a while, if sure feels like you are cooped up in the buildings you live and play in. Make a plan for yourself. Yes, you can always watch television, but get your reading material, and anything that you can focus on, instead of the boredom that will settle in. You'll be limited to going outside, going to work, getting exercise, or having any type of fun. Some campers will find themselves getting under others skin. There is no way to avoid it. When this happens, stay to yourself. Don't get involved with the wintertime drama. Be prepared, someone may say something about you to another camper. Or they may try to engage you in a conversation with them about someone they don't like. Don't fall into that trap. Word travels quickly in a place like this. It's amazing how something so simple can get distorted, blown out of proportion, and anything you say will not be replicated as you said it, trust me on this.

Even though the holidays are tough when you're in camp, by being able to reach out to them will make your time go by quick. Knowing that there is only three weeks until Thanksgiving, then another four weeks until Christmas, you'll become more aware that it won't be long now and you're going home.

I'll be honest, the winter shows things down quite a bit. You can only work out inside. You may find yourself playing more cards. Daylight savings time shortens your day, so you may end up sleeping a little more often. The holidays will come at you quickly. Pay attention, there may be campers who are making thing at your camp. holiday gift type items. You may want to get your order in early for Christmas, it takes forever to get mail out and you don't want it to be late.

You'll be surprised, knitting is a big hobby around here. You can usually get something made pretty cheaply. Plan ahead or better yet, you can create something yourself.

Whatever it is that you can do for yourself, do it. Don't allow those wintertime blues get you down.

Count-Camp

You won't believe the number of times you get counted in a day and at night. You will begin to think you're in a herd of cattle headed to a livestock kill. You'll get used to it, like anything else in here. After a while, it begins to get old. The big joke is that when you get out, you will need someone to come by and count you. You'll feel like it's 1984 and Big Brother is watching. Sure, you cannot wait until it's over. This is part of the system. The BOP is institutionalizing you. Or at least they're attempting to do so. Can you imagine what that's like when you're in for 5, 10, or 20 years? When is enough, enough?

Suspicion- Camp

At some point, you will be going home. Every one of us want it to be sooner than later, especially you. Since you have been convicted with a crime, you'll be the one they look at when things go wrong. You won't want to believe that it could be possible, but how is it that you are always at fault? You're not and you need to believe in yourself. You have admitted responsibility, paid your dues to society, and now it's time to move forward. Time to start a new life. It's possible to do so with your spouse, family, or a friend or two. Or you may just to have to start all over again by choosing a new town to live in, finding new people to associate with, and creating a new you. Don't give anyone any reason to point a finger at you.

If you can, travel clean and avoid any scenes. Don't go anywhere that may draw attention to you. If possible, don't go back into the same line of work. You may be restricted to some degree based on your previous punishment. That would be like suicide, for sure. It may be best to do something different, so there is no question. You want to maintain the highest level of integrity that you can possibly uphold.

They say never to drink and drive. Be the designated driver, but don't drink. Following the law will you back on track to keeping the suspicions down.

You may find yourself wanting to challenge your sentence. There are always campers who will do what they can to get their time reduced or to possibly get out earlier than planned.

2255-Camp

The government has a great way of giving everyone a ray of hope. They may throw a little bit of sunshine your way. They want you to think that there is hope for you, yet.

Keep in mind that there are two types of inmates. One, is the person who just go hung up on doing something bad, such as dealing drugs, who fell up a lot of people, both on the state and federal levels. The prosecutors do not really care about the majority of those type of criminals. Many of them, especially the younger ones, will go to jail, and because of how poor the system is, will eventually return. Maybe this is because selling drugs is the only way that they know how to make money. The percentage of them that have any type of education, or knowledge of a technical trade is at zero. It's tough to be capable of making $5k a week selling drugs then go to $500.00 per week. The system does not do enough to provide better paths or possibilities for success for these folks. It's basically a dead-end situation. Ultimately, they become just another number in the system, and more often than not they get lost in there. During this time, their parole officer will have all of the control of them.

The other type of an inmate is the real target, the white-collar guy, with a high-profile case. His story makes the front page of your local newspaper and is making the headlines on the major news stations. With these cases, it doesn't matter about right or wrong, ethical or not, these are the people that have to be very careful in all that they do.

I thought about a 2255, as many campers will anything to shorten their time or get it overturned. My lawyer, Paul Dull, was a total jerk and did so poorly with regard to my case. He, like many lawyers would do, made a deal with the court, and did not feel any obligation to relate that information to me. I am not sure that he knew what he was doing. Just as countless other lawyers do not know what they are doing, or are just too busy to care. He just collected his money and here I am. I undeniably had a legitimate complaint about my case, and very well have prevailed. However, my friend KC explained to me numerous times how dangerous and risky it is to file a 2255, especially for someone like me, who had a target on his back. Many of these prosecutors would love to put a little cherry on top of this cupcake.

A 2255 Petition may be filed by a person in federal custody to challenge a federal criminal conviction and/or sentence. 28 U.S.C. § 2255 provides that it may be used to raise claims that your sentence or conviction was unauthorized under any law of the United States.

Headline news, the guy I railroaded is headed back because he proclaimed he has ineffective counsel. What nerve he has to question one of our bandits. Who is going to pay for my lunch next week? The prosecutors want you to try them. You it is as simple as this. When they have you. It's not about justice or fairness, it's about me looking good. The government put all that money into investigating you, why would they want to compromise their expenses?

I figure in my case they spent more money in over 10 years of investigating than I owed. It would make too much sense to save the money make a deal and get paid. Having common sense doesn't apply sometimes in the law. Let's cut to the chase and really look at some solutions. With the prisons and camps overflowing with the US leading the world with the highest incarcerated inmates, someone should really give this logic some thought.

Maybe you should think twice about filing a 2255 Petition, even if you're right about your lawyer. Is it best just to accept responsibility and do the time? Once it's done and over with, hopefully you've learned a lesson and can move on with your life. For my friend KC is 74 years old, and 2 years into a 10-year sentence, he has a solid case and nothing to lose. I have less than 10 months to serve and it would be a waste of my time and effort to move forward on a 2255.

You potentially have a lot to lose. Jim, a guy at the camp served about 3 years and fought extremely hard to get his case heard He got out and went to a halfway house, when they arrested him on a new charge. He's back at the camp serving a few more years, and he's fighting it again, claiming his innocence, again. The bottom line is that if the government wants to put your mother in jail, they can succeed in doing so. Does it make any sense that I ask that you out there and fight an uphill battle? You really need to think the process through and make your own intelligent decision. We haven't mentioned the cost. Some guys go to jail and the first thing on their agenda is how they're going to get out. They plan to beat the system. Is that what got them there to begin with in the first place. Just be cautious and wise about things. It's you against the government. How is that you really can beat them at their game?

Take a moment and think about the cost that you will now accumulate. You're not using your old attorney, and you have to hire a new one. What is that going to run you, $5k, $10k, to $15k? Cases can run into the 100,000.00 of dollars and for what? It may not be more time than a civil case of evicting someone from a dwelling space. Whatever the expense, it's going to be costly. You have to have the money and be willing to take that risk. No, thanks for the offer, but I think I will pass. Lawyers like to make deals. Many of them won't get all of the information that is needed to try your case. The fees they charge are outrageous, and you feel thought your story should be explained. Mine was not told. My lawyer rolled over. He was just horrible. My personal plan is to file a law suit against my former incompetent attorney Paul Dull and practice. I plan on getting him where it hurts. This is one way to skin that cat.

There are so many folks that will work with the in house, convict home-spun "lawyers" that will fill their heads with ideas, pipe dreams, and anything that to get their time reduced or to get them out. In our camp, KC put in countless hours for many inmates. There is usually one such person in the USP system. KC has helped so many campers, more than you can imagine. He toils at their 2255 Petitions, motions of all types, including the reduction of sentencing due to the guidelines of the law. He starts at 5:30 in the morning and except for breakfast, lunch, and dinner, he works 'til 8:30 at night, helping out the other campers. It doesn't matter who they are or what they have done, he helps them. He asks for nothing in return. Will it surprise you to know that maybe one or two would actually be gracious enough to buy him some whiteout or typewriter ribbon for the typewriter? No, the only person that's actually done something like that for him, has been me. They scream for help over and over, but just like in their outside lives, many are not appreciative of someone going out of their way, at their own expense, and with care to help them get their freedom. What is it worth to you to have your freedom? How about some gratitude and appreciation?

Once you are in for a little bit, you will realize that everyone has a story, and every reason has been wronged. Someone did something to them and they are innocent. There is no accountability, no responsibility. You've probably heard the old adage, heard one story, and have heard them all. You sure may be a little sympathetic to a story, but the big picture tells you that they're where they're at for a reason. So, be smart with your decisions, ok?

Appeal

Do you have a big case, one that could be appealed? Did you think that you can appeal a plea? Did you take your case to court and risk the increase in the number of years that the prosecutors like to threaten with you? We can put you in jail with your mother for 30 years. Really, are you kidding? What is the best option for me? Sounds simple, or so you would think.

Attorneys will charge upwards of $20k, be sure of this. Do you have any idea of how long the process actually is? Would you be surprised if told you it will take anywhere from 3-5 years. If you have a 5-year sentence, is it even worth it? My friend Freddy has 10 years and has completed two. His case is under appeal at this moment. He has a great case to appeal, with the resources for the perfect appeal. The government has worked hard to stall the appeal by creating postponement after postponement. By doing this, they are asking for more time.

Why do you think the government gives extensions to the prosecutions but gives nothing to you? You will be expected to rise to the highest level to perform properly but not the government. Your tax paying dollars being spent wisely, not!

The District Court will not want to hear your case again. That's the last thing they want, a black eye. All you want is a fair and equitable hearing that you claim that you did not receive. That's going to be difficult to get a second time around, won't it? Especially if you are forced to look at the case, when it concerns facts about the law or procedure. If you have a lot of time and money and you're truly correct, and I do mean 100% correct, then you should definitely consider a second shot at achieving your freedom. You never want to give up, it's what keeps you going. It allows you the ability to sleep at night, as well as gives you a reason to get up in the morning. It will give you a lot to talk about with the other campers that you will become friends with. Maybe someone has a similar story and you can help one another.

Just like anything else, be careful of what you wish for, you may just get it. I think the government keeps an ace in their pocket. If you go after them in an appeal, a motion, or a 2255 Petition, they may end up booking the case, but they have that ace that they will use and go after you again. You want that to ever happen to you. So be careful.

Speaking of the government …

The Government

The government gets a hold of you and won't let go. You may or may not have done anything but your choice is 30 years in prison or you can take a plea with two years. What is that you will chose? There is a trend showing that prosecutors make up evidence to make their cases look good, and they advance their careers while doing so. Guess what, you're going to prison and they're profiting from it. My question that I continuously raise is, when will these prosecutors start getting prosecuted for their crimes? Is this a conspiracy? You wouldn't believe how many people I have met that are doing a lot of time for conspiracy, why aren't some them prosecuting attorneys? The government will scare the hell out of you so that you're forced to take a deal. Most of us do not want to spend an eternity in the USP, not one of us wants to risk that.

During your time at any government institution, whether it be a camp, maximum or minimum security, or any level of the government facilities or offices, you are meant to receive a real education, and you will. You may be one of those people that can accept how and why the government works the way it does. I have found the true meaning of using five people to dig one small hole. That level of incompetency takes me to new levels each day. How is it that the motivated and educated are paid so well that we have some level of efficiency and order? What about the majority of people who just want to get by with the least that they can do?

What about the whistle blowers? They are certainly not exposed to you. Many parts of the government are unionized and don't do a great job in promoting a balanced equal employment opportunity. The government workers that I have seen at the BOP seem to have high paid menial jobs. They also receive great benefits along with that great pay. Instead of using some level of sensibility, they will allow for gross overtime and complacency. What kind of job can you get where you are paid to sit around all day doing nothing or play solitaire? Not many, or at least not in USP have enough sense.

Can you imagine taking a job and your primary responsibility is to count grown men at 10 AM, 4 PM, 9 PM, 3 AM, and 5 AM? That's pretty much all you do in a day besides that, you keep yourself alive and do your best to stay awake when you get bored. Some people question why the government doesn't have much money, or better yet, too much money that they really don't know how to spend. Someone should care, but they don't. If they did, our government would be lean and mean.

A small business in the US could not operate in this fashion, it would go belly up within a year. The smart government workers and there are plenty of them, quit after 20 years of services so that they can collect their retirement. They typically start consulting firms or go to work for one and do the same job that they just left with the government, for triple the pay. Something is wrong with this picture. Hey, it's the government, which is so big and over protected that people have to learn to accept it for what it is. There are new prisons all over the country but they can't open them due to a tight budget with issues. There is little money to pay the right people to run these joints, let alone the operating equipment, cars, office supplies, etc. They build them because years before someone for the expense put through as budgetary expense items, and boom, there you go!

Pre-Trial- Camp

The longer I am at the camp, the more people I talk with, the more I realize that the pre-trial for your alleged crime will be the worst that you will have to deal with. It won't be easy. The government loves to mess with your mind. No matter what you are charged with, consider yourself as one worst of the worst in the government's eyes. They may let you out on bond, but with restrictions, which I recommend that you follow as closely as possible. If there is any question about extenuating circumstances, they may put you under house arrest, and bless you with an ankle bracelet. They may allow you to go to work, go to church, or to your doctor, but will keep you locked down in your house, otherwise. This is tough to deal with, but better than the alternative.

If they want to squeeze you and make your life miserable, they will lock you up in a county jail. This is an uncomfortable experience that I am certain you will never forget. Most likely you'll be there with criminals of all types, many for very bad crimes. Eventually you'll go your separate ways. From this point it can only get better, right?

It's hard to wrap your mind around something that you know nothing about, or what to expect. The prosecutors are threatening you with a lot of time, they throw out numbers like 10 years to 30 years, and make it sound like it's just a month or two. Perhaps this is just how they operate, and if that's the case, there's no way around it. You accept it and learn how to deal with it. Everyone handles things in their own way or may have a different attitude than the next. You'll be stuck and keep talking about it, when you're in the camp. Most people facing this are intimidated by this.

There may be a greater chance for some people of going into a county jail for holding until your court date. You'll experience all of the moves, such as being in leg locked shackles, having a little black box around your wrists while making your way to court. It will not be easy to forget, walking into a courtroom wearing a jail uniform. Many places will place you in a courthouse holding cell, and may take the cuffs off. This is surely a very low point in one's life. I know it was for me. It doesn't get much lower than that. Fortunately, when you arrive at the camp, you will not observe any type of this activity. You'll be free to walk around, even if you go to the big house for a medical exam. You won't be shackled up.

Even if you're guilty for the charges that have been brought up against you, it appears to be a game that the government plays with you. They don't care to understand that this is serious business to you or me and you don't appreciate the game. Anyone who has never been through such a process is going to understand how serious it is. Many of those who have made this their career will not. Maybe that's who the system has been designed for.

It would be nice to think that there should be some major reform to this system, especially since the government is over 15 trillion dollars in debt and is growing daily. Isn't there someone within the system that maybe thinking that what they are doing is wrong and there is a need for change? I can't help but to wonder why a guy who did not pay his taxes or a guy who sold a little crack is treated the same way someone who has felled 10 innocent people. Why is it that nobody sees the difference? Most people who have been convicted of a crime, understand pretty quickly. Spend six months in a county jail or in a camp and you will understand the severity of what you have done. Let them go home, work, pay taxes, even participate in community service. To take them out of society for five years or even ten years. It's like we're living in the dark ages. If you give someone a break, then give them some rope. If they hang themselves, then let them hang. Someone who has learned his lesson isn't going to be stupid enough to sell drugs again.

My offense involved payroll taxes. I have no interest in having an employee again. I plan on helping businesses that need to understand how the payroll tax system works, be diligent and forthright in running their businesses. This is a great plan for me.

Did I Mention Fog Count?

Fog Count

Are you kidding me? What is a fog count? That's what it is, what's crazy is that most of the people here could not say their "g's" so it sounded a lot like "fall count". Half the people around here are wondering just what a fog count even is. We waited and waited, but nobody came around to do a count. Come to find out, it was not a fall count, but a fog count. Where there is so much fog and the COs can't see in front of them, they do a count. Even though the inmates are all in place, lets count them up.

Mind Your Own Business- Camp

This is going to be tough for you, me, and the guy next door. Just try to remember to mind your own business. You will have a lot of time to widdle away. There will be little to talk about. Of course, you will still talk to some people, share some stories, and for some, just talk about anything to anyone. To be honest, I would say that for the most part, most of that talking is just a total waste of time because everyone has their own story and cares pretty much only for themselves. Many campers are just trying to figure out who they are, what they are going to do next, and what's going to happen once they get out. A drug dealer who has made huge amounts of money before, does not want to get into that business when he is released. So, the question is, will he be able to go to work at a regular 8:00-5:00 job? Will he show up every day? How will he adjust to a lower level of pay? It certainly will pale in comparison to what he used to make. That's been spent! He really wants to change. Most people would bet that although he says he wants to change, that he does not have the work ethic to succeed and that he will not be satisfied with his new wage. The economy is bad and unemployment is at a record high. It's going to become less than none that anyone without a real solid connection will be able to find a decent job.

Many of these guys that you will meet are afraid of falling back into what they left behind. These guys would primarily be those who are dealing drugs, that absolutely knew that they were breaking the law and it was just a matter of time before they got caught. I will have to say, I haven't seen too many people trying to connect in camp so that they are able to get back into the drug business when they get out. I would suggest that they get back into it, not only because of ignorance, but because of greed, not knowing the difference between right and wrong, but also not having the other tools that are necessary for their own success.

They must have a support system that can keep them grounded and totally committed to taking the right path. That path may not be quick and provide immediate results that you may be expecting. You may need things, as your family, you may have obligations to pay, as well as an array of other expenses. Just remember that these things, all of them, do not have to be paid today. Put these on the back shelf. Establish a priority list of the most important ones, which maybe you and your family first, then the other items that you want to take care of. Make your money honestly and then attack that list. Don't get yourself wrapped up in a mess.

What's been interesting to watch, are the scammers. You will see conmen working the campers at the camp. What they did on the outside, some consider this their magic, they will do on the inside. There is no remorse. They will find weaker inmates, who they will show them or promise them a dream to work towards, and they will rope them in. You may want to keep bust but don't stick yourself out there to be taken advantage of!

I wonder how you would be able to borrow a couple of million dollars to start a trucking company? Do you really think that with a bad economy, that there is a lot of need for hauling? What's really bad, is when campers come in, and when they leave, they've been raped by the government and have nothing but a huge pile of bills, bad credit and the inability to borrow $100.00. The guys that purposely took money from their victims and blame it on someone else are my favorites. These people come into a camp, they lie about what they did, and it does not take them long to find people to go after on the inside. It's really sad to see. During my time in the camp, I saw several people putting together business plans. All of those that I saw seemed to be so unrealistic, or illegal. They appeared to be something that would take time out of your day to prepare for. There was one guy who was developing a liquidation market for pharmaceuticals. This was so far out of touch, as it would cost over $100k to build the site. While he was on his anti-depressant medication, he was able to cut out little pictures and put them on a well-designed website.

You want to be realistic with your dreams. Don't turn your dreams into fantasies that just out of reach. You want to be able to wrap your hands around what you want to go after. Keep yourself grounded so that when you get out, you can jumpstart your idea and get moving with it. You just wasted a portion of your life, don't waste any more time trying to climb a greasy pole. You can't make progress when you do this.

What's worked for me is holding a regular job, reading some current sports news, and writing. I am always curious about the drama that goes on. I listen but try not to ask too many questions or give anyone the impression that I care. You really don't want to care. You just want your time to go by and do so quickly. Keep your distance. You will figure quickly who to chat with and who to stay away from.

Think what you do say to others thoroughly as it can come back and bite you in the butt. Keep in mind that this is not a popularity contest. You know that you will probably never see any of these people in here again. You may have one or two that you will choose to keep up with once you are back on the outside. Just remember if you hear something or see something, just keep your mouth shut and mind your own business.

"Sweep in front of your own door" – German Proverb

Sex-Camp

The topic of sex in an USP confinement can be an awkward or embarrassing one of some, but it's one of those topics that just can't be left out of this guide for what to expect.

We've all watched plenty of prison movies and television shows. Since we just don't know what really is, we are genuinely concerned or nervous about what we may be walking into. Especially in a USP camp. We've shared some stories about what goes on beyond the wall, especially in maximum security facilities. Hopefully this will set your mind at ease.

I'm here to tell you to relax. Nobody is going to attack you when you walk into the camp. The camps are not filled with men who have a homosexual orientation. Most likely, you may not even witness anything. Let me be clear; however, it may be a different story for a self-surrender than it is for a step-down guy. Most of the step-down inmates know what to expect. They know how to behave for the most part, and what they can get away with say, and what they can't. I think for the most part, many of them have an attitude to begin with. This is laughable, but during the time I was at the camp, I only observed a few inmates who I truly believed earned the reward of being there. Most of the rest needed a serous bout with reality.

When you are entering the camp for the first time, it's like you are walking into a fresh new world with no idea of what you are going to have the opportunity to experience. Don't worry about this too much. The camps need a diversity of people. It would appear to me that they want to mix the two groups together. The self- surrenders do not need the step-down guys. I will say that the mix brings a level of stability into the camp. I must say, it's quite the mix of people. The socio-economic and cultural differences could just about choke a horse. I spend a lot of time shaking my head. I've asked myself repeatedly, "what am I doing here?" I've said to myself a million times, "Are you kidding me? How did I ever stoop so low? How could I have been so stupid to put myself in this type of situation?" So here I am, now I have to dance to the tune that we're playing on the jukebox. You may experience the same, once you've been here a few weeks, and see what I mean.

Most of the step-down guys are here due to dealing drugs. Most of the self-surrenders are here because of a white-collar crime they've committed. To be honest, most of them are here because the government puts so much pressure on you to take a plea bargain and avoid going to trial. Who in their right mind wants to risk getting double or triple more time? Many of us find ourselves convinced to just get it done and over with. You have your conspirators and probation/parole violators that have a little more or less than a year to serve. In most cases, it seems like a money and time waster! Seems to me some of these guys could have served their time in the county jail for 60-days, or be placed on house arrest.

Getting back to the topic of sex…yes, there are some gay inmates at the camp. Most of them will be in the closet and behave like they're in the closet, even though they are not. Quite frankly, they are more intimidated than you are. They are completely freaked out about what they are coming into. Which I promise you, is not much. As I mentioned, you won't have to worry much. Most of the fellows who are gay lay pretty low. They stay under the radar. It would not be comfortable for them to announce to the group that they are gay. Now I will have to say, you may recognize that one gay inmate may inadvertently or unknowingly sell another out. One day I heard Tom say to someone else, "Hey, he is one of us!" They typically stay to themselves and are relatively quiet. There are some step-downs that may go both ways, thinking whatever that they do in the camp stays in the camp and nobody on the outside will ever know.

The best thing to do is stay to yourself, avoid having discussions that involve homosexual content. Unless you have the orientation, it's another one of those situations you don't want to waste your time or effort on. There will be some homophobes but you won't know who's pitching, who's catching, or who is on first. This is always for the best. If you hang out with people who are similar to you, you'll be okay. You won't find anyone making a private tent it their bunk space so they have sex. Nobody will be jumping into your bunk with you. You may find yourself tested, but usually not. There is no chance of you being pimped out. You won't have to be concerned about having to defend yourself. You're in a safe place. The shower is always private and maybe the best place for your personal business.

I heard a story tonight at Jimmy's going away party. When Drew camp to the camp, like most, he was told not to eat or drink anything while on the bus, because using the toilet is very difficult. You don't get much sleep and may still be stunned by the recent changes in your life. Or should I say, shocked? It's just a crazy transition. Drew arrives at the camp. He's a clean-cut dude.

He gets the top bunk and attempts to sleep for the next three days. At some point during this time, he peers over his bunk to look down the hallway, lined with bunks and campers. He sees Johnny. He's completely beat and doesn't know anyone. Johnny is sitting a few bunks from him, sitting in a chair, knitting a pink bear for someone. Johnny is very strong, with huge muscles. He's wearing a wife beater t-shirt, shorts, and only his top teeth, which are actually dentures. He rarely speaks to anyone, not even a hello. Drew was scared out of his mind, not the government issue over his head. Who wouldn't be? He decided to sleep for another day. He could not quite wrap his head around what he got himself involved in, who he was surrounded by, and why he was even there. It wasn't his crowd on the outside.

Johnny works in welding. We actually have become good friends and I wouldn't mind him working for me because he's very talented. He has 10 years down and is ready to go home. Since I am they payroll clerk in the welding shop and this pay period, I am going to try to get him a bonus, as well as his vacation pay. Why not? He knits to pass the time and to make a little extra cash. Everything he makes, he sends home to support his family. What a gentleman! Six months later, he and Drew are lifting weights together, even though Johnny still rarely speaks to anyone.

It's nice to have one person to connect with, to hang out with, and not have to worry about anything outside of the ordinary happening. I found a few months ago that Johnny who was in prison for dealing drugs went right back into business when he was released. This time he was caught with a gun in his possession. This is a big-time problem for a to begin with. It's an automatic 5 years, mandatory. Why did he take the risk? He also had a variety of drugs on him. He may find himself a life sentence at this point because he's a repeat offender. All I know is that is it won't be easy for you when you get back on the outside, but I encourage you to do your best to stay in your own lane, be the best you can be, and don't put yourself at risk, ever!

There haven't been any transgender people in the camp. Since I've been here, there has only been one guy that was considered a flamer. His name was Larry. He would dance around and show his flare. He's not a threat to anyone, nobody really cares, and most campers may just laugh at him, as it's pretty comical to see. We still talk about him.

So no, matter which way you come in, or which way you go or don't go, don't worry about any crazy prison movie activity happening. It most likely will never happen.

There are some experiences that you really should be advised of. This is for not only your safety, but for your peace of mind.

Grievance (Lunch Out)- Camp

You never want to organize yourself with a group of campers or inmates to complain to anyone about anything, because it is really considered as a form of a riot. This will get you into big time trouble. If anything were ever to occur, you want to be careful who you talk to and about what. Whoever has the idea should be someone who has been around for a while. Someone who knows what they are doing. Not that it takes knowledge, or that age is a factor to pull it off. Having some experience and maturity always helps in any situation. You want to have that if the camp has any grievances, you will need to follow protocol. You never want to anything that will get you or anyone else in any type of trouble.

Keep in mind that the case manager at any camp or USP is the gatekeeper to your freedom. He is responsible for keeping up with your case. He is responsible for team meetings, as well as completing the paperwork that is necessary for your release. You do want to go home, don't you? The old guards in the BOP system, as well as many civilians, believe that no matter what you have done wrong in life, that they should lock you up and throw away the key. That's not how it should work today. How many people just crossed the line by mistake. They may have been pulled into something, tormented, threatened, or bribed, along with a number of other situations that created them to step over the line, and put them in a bad situation. Many of them are genuinely good people, just like you and me. There are others in the BOP system that want you to go home. Our case manager, West, apparently doesn't want anyone to go home, ever. How is that possible? You may ask. I'm here to tell you it is. He has failed at having team meetings, failed at following BOP procedures. He's even failed at providing basic rights. You are paying your price to society. There are some people, I want to say, that got pulled over in line and did not get caught. I don't feel too bad if you're one of those people with a mindful purpose, that had victims that got serious hurt, either physically or financially. Stealing other people's money is never okay, is it?

There are many regulations and different ways for an inmate to get out of camp. You get a good time, home confinement, halfway house, or even a drug program, just to name a few. Each reason has a different set of circumstances that can pave the road to freedom. It's up to the case manager to look at your PSI and figure out what is best for you. At this moment, there are over 20,000 convicted citizens and step-down candidates that need to go to a camp. There is a waiting list, isn't that hard to believe? At the rate that the government continues to severely punish light citizen "criminals", and considering the prosecutors are gunslingers, there will be an unnecessary need for continued growth of the BOP system. I say unnecessary because it is unnecessary. It makes better sense to eliminate senseless and frivolous government spending by creating new sentencing guidelines, creating reform opportunities for crimes that require minimal reform, and save the prisons and camps for the hard crimes. It's a no brainer, really.

Everyone wants to go home and be with their family, so let's work towards that. West was not interested in making that happen. He constantly fails to submit any paperwork in on time for the campers. He just doesn't care, it's all a matter of collecting a paycheck and going home. He also lies constantly and to everyone. At first, I just thought everyone was being really hard on him, but that's not the case. It's plain as day. He just didn't care about his job or anyone and did nothing. You would be amazed if you knew how many people that work for the government and do nothing. You can work for the government and have plenty of time to scour the internet, play Sudoku, and even pursue other careers. Nobody cares! You would think that there would be someone accountable for supervising and auditing to catch the wasted time and payroll. Apparently, there is not. What ever happened to coming to work to work? We could have been a crossword puzzle master for all I know. He's just one of the many apathetic people who get the privilege to work for the government, but not actually work.

Wouldn't you know it, word got out around the camp that nobody at the camp, that is 152 campers, were going to lunch. It's interesting because one thing that the government does monitor is how many meals they serve at each facility. Hey, people have to eat and they want to know if you're indeed eating or not. You don't want to have an "eat out" often. It will get everyone's attention. In most places, they scan your ID card so they have a record. Your grievance should be worthy. That being said, a new TV or softballs are not worth the effort. This particular problem with West preventing people from going home is worth it.

The way this works is that you do an "eat out" on the day that has the best meal of the week. For us, that is a Thursday when we have chicken. Everyone likes chicken. This is what we did. Nobody organized it, there was no leader. You don't want to have a leader. Word went around the camp pretty quickly. Some of the brothers had to be convinced not to eat. Eddie was good about getting the word out and he made sure it got around. The word spread Wednesday into Wednesday night. Thursday came and at 10:30, everyone started to hang out in front of the chow hall. We waited and waited. One of the AW's, a congressman, and a few of the COs wandered through the camp. This was a political visit, how appropriate. The main line was closed, so we managed a great opportunity to make a statement. Mike was late for work so lunch was late. 11:15 came, the AW and visitors were gone, the main line was called and everyone at the camp stood outside of the chow hall. Nobody made a move to go in and eat. What a great feeling to have everyone on the same page, supporting this effort. We were making a statement and it was all good.

We continued to wait. A few of the COs went into the chow hall to get their lunch. When they came out, they looked around, smiled, and kept walking. We were stilling waiting and another half an hour passed by when Ms. G, the administrator for the SFF and camp suddenly appeared. With her was McCall, the camp counselor and a few other COs were behind them. Ms. G is tough, strong, but professional. She asked us if anyone were hungry and thought that we had made a mistake in our tactics. We stood firm with our decision. She shared with me at a time when people who wanted to speak could do so. Several of the guys, at least 15 of them told her their stories, and they were all worthy, legitimate, and consistent. They told her how West just lied to them and refused to do any of their paperwork. She heard the message loud and clear. She told everyone that she was going to solve the problem. She instructed everyone to email her a request to meet to explain their situations, this was the standard protocol. She promised she would each of their requests.

She told us that West had been doing nothing, of which we already knew, and he was not ever going to do anything. He was now going to be eliminated from the equation. We liked what we were hearing. She was taking a level of responsibility, as she opened the door for us, as campers, to go directly to her with our issues. She was surprised and almost upset that nobody had received any relief from the Second Chance Act. The Second Chance Act (SCA) supports state, local, and tribal governments and nonprofit organizations in their work to reduce recidivism and improve outcomes for people returning from state and federal prisons, local jails, and juvenile facilities. Passed with bipartisan support and signed into law on April 9, 2008, and reauthorized in 2018, SCA legislation authorizes federal grants for vital programs and systems reform aimed at improving the reentry process.[16] There were 85 campers that were eligible for halfway houses, but only one had paperwork processed. Most campers were not receiving any of their "good time" or their "at home confinement time". There was no consistency to any of the procedures that are outlined in the BOP handbook.

The more she listened, you could see she was getting angrier and angrier. That was okay, she should be angry. By the way, she has a pleasant look about her, and you could see that morphing into twisted frustration. Once the discussions were finished, everyone went to lunch. All the fuss over a piece of chicken that was the size of a pigeon's leg, but lunch is lunch, we were hungry, so we had no problems gobbling that down.

I am personally eligible for something with 38 weeks left. West had told me no halfway house or Second Chance Act. Guess what West, you provided me with the wrong answer. I immediately sent Ms. G a request to staff, a thank you note for her time, and requested a halfway house. In my request I asked her to complete my paperwork as soon as those that had been waiting longer were complete. Many campers were long overdue to be sent home or to receive a benefit from the Second Chance Act. Johnny, Jeff, and John were just a few that I knew. I was fine waiting for them to receive what they have been long waiting for. I knew I could wait for that to happen with no problem.

---

[16] https://nationalreentryresourcecenter.org/second-chance-act

When I finished my email request to Ms. G, I helped 4 others get theirs done because they either couldn't write or use type. I took them to the warehouse and made copies. All was good. I had done my job and was happy to do so.

I heard through the grapevine that Ms. G went to West and gave him hell. Apparently, he had the guts to snap back at her, which led to her telling him in so many words that she could easily move him out of his position, that he needed to be complete, and he did. I saw him leave the camp that day around 2:30. He was looking for the most part like a wounded puppy. Someone should have kicked him out the door on his way out. She then brought her team to the USP and met with the warden. You know he has to know what's going on here, but maybe didn't know to what degree, or maybe he just didn't care? I heard it was a good meeting. There was a buzz in the air around the camp. Many of us short timers started to get a little excited that there was some relief coming our way. The old timers were a little more skeptical.

The sunset that night was quite nice, the mood was a little more relaxed, as it appeared some relief was near. We were happy. The workers went to work the next day. It was Labor Day weekend. It was going to be my last Labor Day weekend at the camp. I was ready to get it going and done with. Roland, my son, said he was going to come to see me in the morning. I have heard that before, only to have a no show, so I really had no idea if he was coming or not.

At 8:30 on that Friday, we were told that the warden, Terry, was coming to the camp to talk to us. Hopefully, this would be good news. I felt that it was going to be, no doubt in my mind. He was a few minutes late and as he walked out to the courtyard, one of the campers, Kevin, who was extremely anxious blurted out something. The warden did not like that one bit. He flexed his muscles, called him out on it, and had him sent to the location. Man, was that a use of power. Ok, Mr. Warden, we get it, you made your point, now what's the news? By the way, Kevin was released after the meeting.

The warden apologized for the interruption, the problems everyone had been experiencing, and told us that he would take care of everything. He told us that he would be sending people to the camp next week to get all of the paperwork needed completed. I believed this would happen, he seemed serious about this. He appears to be a professional. He genuinely seemed to want to us to rejoin our families. He explained that any and all time off, whether it be good time, a halfway house, or even a drug program, if you were entitled to the benefit, you were going to receive it, or if you weren't entitled, you would have an answer as to why not. He wasn't going to let anyone hang around waiting. There were new campers that needed to come in and he wanted to get the process going as quickly as possible.

He joked around about cell phones and alcohol, as he usually does. We all know it doesn't do him any good to keep people in the camp. It's time for some of us to go home. He said all of the right things, and I think he meant it. Hopefully, he's opened the doors to making some changes, to putting an end to the bullshit, and getting some campers home to their families. There was absolutely no motivation to hurt anyone, or keep them retained.

This was probably one of the only productive experiences that took place while I was in the camp.

Quick Facts

1. Before filing a lawsuit, an inmate MUST complete the grievance process. Therefore, it is important that all prisoners with a grievance start and complete the process as soon as possible.
2. Grievances must include as much detail as possible, including specific names, dates, and facts
3. A grievance must be filed within 60 days of the incident giving rise to the complaint.
4. If an inmate does not receive a response at any stage of the process, he/she should move along to the next step in the process, including a note as to why the prior stage was not completed
5. If filing a grievance about a facility other than the one where the prisoner is currently incarcerated, the grievance can be sent directly to the ARB.
6. It's VERY important to keep notes and records of any communications with prison staff about the status of grievances. [17]

---

[17] https://www.ilnd.uscourts.gov/_assets/_documents/_forms/_paveyhearing/IDOC%20 Grievance%20Proc.%20summary.pdf

I've included a copy of a grievance form that's used in the system. As simple as this form is, there is a process to everything.

```
BP-A0176                    FORMAL GRIEVANCE FORM    CDFRM
JUN 10
U.S. DEPARTMENT OF JUSTICE                    FEDERAL BUREAU OF PRISON


1. Grievant(s)                          2. Duty Station


3. Representative of Grievant(s)        4. Informal resolution attempted with (name Person)


5. Federal Prison System Directive, Executive Order, or Statute violated:



6. In what way were each of the above violated? Be specific.




7. Date(s) of violation(s)




8. Request remedy (i.e., what you want done)



9. Person with whom filed                10. Title

11. Signature of recipient               12. Date signed

I hereby certify that efforts at informal resolution have been unsuccessful.
13. Signature of Grievant(s)             14. Signature of Representative


Record Copy - Agency; Copy - Union Local; Copy - Council of Prison Locals; Copy - Grievant



PDF                    Prescribed by P3713              This form replaces BP-176(37)
                                                        Dated October 1984.
```

As you grow older, you begin to notice that life is pretty much consistent and repetitive. We get up in the morning, have coffee, eat some breakfast, go to work, come home eat dinner, watch some TV, go to bed, only to do it all over again the next day. Of course, many people have extra-curricular activities in between. Some of us may exercise, some may enjoy cocktail hour, and others may travel around a little bit here and there.

Gratitude

Success is inevitable with self-appreciation and being generous. Preserve your knowledge and be generous with your heart. Take time to say thank you to the people who have assisted you with your success. Be firm and fair but extend gratitude when it is deserving. Don't forget that you are a good person. For years, other's perceptions of me have not been good. I've never felt comfortable with that, but most people either owed me money or I had to have their car towed from my properties. Hey, what do you expect? Either way, what someone may think and what is reality are typically two different things. I have been more than gracious my entire life. I've always put others first and taken the back seat. I've never minded doing so. I've always settled on the silver instead of the gold. Being second best and not in first place was just how I rolled. Being second best is just fine in the eyes of God, because you are living your life the right way, which I always did, and am proud of it. I feel as though I have helped a lot of people with giving them assistance with their careers, build their families, and changed the course of their lives. You can do the same. A small amount of kindness and generosity will go a long way. You just have to make your move and do it. I have no regrets for any of my kindness and generosity, and you shouldn't either.

I cannot count the number of people who have taken advantage of my acts of kindness and generosity and have considered them a sign of weakness. Go figure, I thought that was part of human nature, but I guess not. I have spent a whole life time giving to others without considering myself. I've learned though that it's important to think of yourself and your family from time to time. You can't neglect yourself or your family, it will backfire on you. If you're strong, you will not project negativity.

You can make a difference in someone's life, whether it is big or small, it's very meaningful.

Helping someone in need will bring a smile to your heart and it will show up on your face. While you may not feel that great today, tomorrow may be different. God knows what we do and how you've impacted someone else's life. It's a small step with a huge effect. Afterall, that's what it is all about, serving others. Think about the movie, "It's a Wonderful Life", with Jimmy Stewart. It reflects how important each day is and how are lives can be. Through our own heartache and pain, we can provide a bit of goodness to someone, even during the times when others see you as the bad guy.

Consistent- Camp

Everything is almost too consistent in camp. If your camp is like the one that I'm at, people will come and go. You go to work, then you come back. If you don't work, then you will embellish in your routine.

I have this friend in the camp, Bud, who was handed 8 years. He's found his niche, as it is. He's become very comfortable here. Bud is an orderly at the USP on the weekends. This job consists of cleaning for an hour on Saturday or Sunday mornings. He maintains both inside and outside. He gets paid pretty well, but more importantly he stays out of the temporary work details. This means he doesn't get volunteered for crazy jobs, like lockdowns, shoveling snow, or picking up trash. If you're not careful, they will present a list with just about everything you don't want to do on it. The only thing missing is the ball and chain.

During the week, Bud works very hard on his Bible study he has at the camp. His material includes the study of Jesus and the 100 most important things and events that occurred during his life. It's been a huge task for Bud, but it's something he's passionate about. There are plenty of religious resources available in camp, in addition to Bud's awesome Bible study. I told him he should organize it in book form and have it published. It would be a great piece and would serve many well. He agreed and said he's thought about it many times. Why he hasn't done so, I am not sure. Maybe he will once he gets home. No matter what you do to pass your time, find something that is meaningful and will help you.

You'll find that one day rolls into the next and you don't realize one has even passed. For some, it appears that your time will go fast, for some it feels like it's at a snail's pace. You miss your home and loved ones. It's impossible to control anything that's happening on the outside.

Before I came to the camp, I thought I had everything in order, well as much as I thought I had it in order. I had a respectable portfolio of real estate that I gave to my children. They were essentially no help with it and obviously didn't want anything to do with it because it was at a standstill. I didn't understand why. There was no connection to the portfolio and why I was in camp. I had to rely on friends to help and they were willing until they realized how difficult it would be to manage. Well, it was going to be just as difficult for me being on the inside, just about everything is. You can only sit on the sidelines and complain about how the job is being done, only feeling like you could do better. It was very frustrating for me. What was extremely stressful for me was that it was only two weeks in, when they thought they knew better and started changing things. Within months, the communication stopped. It eventually fell apart. They contacted my son Roland, who was a first-year law student, who also thought he knew more than me. Because the communication was non-existent, I had no idea what was going on. You obviously can't run a business while you're inside a camp or prison, but you can protect your interests. The best you can only do is teach, guide, and direct someone you trust. Make sure it's someone you can trust.

While I was in this tough spot, I realized, I've been stripped of all of my assets, my home, cars, and financial resources. This realization makes things a lot easier because you have to let go of it. There is nothing you can do about it. I've met others in the camp that are in the same position. They have small businesses that eventually suffer. Many should go on a hiatus for a while. My situation was a little different because I had nothing. The only interest I had was to provide something substantial for my children, as any parent would. It was important to me that they had a moderate source of income. You may question how bad can it possibly get it while you're away for a few months. For some it can be tremendous, others will find a sense of relief, and even others will find it a way of life. One way to look at it is, if you have to do a year plus a day or less, look at it as an unplanned vacation. Do yourself a favor and prepare the best you can. The shorter time in, the faster it will hopefully go, and you have a better chance of holding on to your life on the outside. If you have more than 36 months, wrap your arms around that large tree, and hug it while you settle in. Hold onto your family, if you have one, as best as you can. It's really the only thing you have.

It was really sad for me because I personally did not have much family support. It really made it difficult to get through the days and weeks, especially at first. For some campers, it was the extreme opposite. They received weekly visits, sometimes even two. It's sad, you will see many campers that have the support they need, many do not. I was lucky that I received one during the year. I can only wait and see how the next 26 weeks will work out for me, maybe I'll get a visit or two. Once you get past the pain because you're not receiving the family support you desperately need, you will be okay. There are some campers that don't want their families to come for a visit. They prefer that they stay home and take care of themselves. It can get quite expensive, some families have to travel well over an hour or so, many even further, so there's time involved. That's quite a commitment.

It's hard on the children, if you have any. If you have any children and they are young, maybe it's simpler to treat this as an out-of-town work assignment. When you have teenage children and young adults, it's harder to conceal what's really going on. It's a difficult time for all of you. I know it was extremely difficult for me. I still think that my three children were deeply embarrassed. They were far from supportive. I have met guys whose children who are older and they understand and are supportive in every aspect. They've stepped up to take care of business, family, phone calls, send letter, you name it. It was great to see. Bud would agree that some are fortunate to have that family support.

People in the camp say that the closer your friends and family are to the camp, the more visits you may receive. I agree that this most likely true, makes sense. It's still a commitment and a sacrifice that our loved ones on the outside have to be willing to make. My friend Mike doesn't get many visits during the year from his family or any friends. He's a really great guy. His daughter's basketball coach visits with Mike once a week. He gives him all of the updates from school, basketball, etc. The discuss her progress on the team. I have been gauging how quickly the months are passing by how often the coach visits with Mike. He usually comes on a Saturday and has been consistent. What a nice guy!

Plan for the worst and hope you get some better than the worst, which would be great! Get the visitation forms sent out and see who will actually show up. I hope you're pleasantly surprised. Do yourself a favor and don't allow yourself to get bitter if it doesn't turn out like you hoped it would. Don't become bitter. Don't hold any grudges.

I had lined up a place to go for a few months once I got out. It's what you call home detention time. I had clothes there and all of my hygiene toiletries, and other necessities. If you're not able to go back to your family, it's always a good idea to have a Plan B ahead of time. Don't attempt to coordinate this effort from the camp. Keep in mind that most people have their own lives, their own situations, and really don't care to associate with you. You'll be surprised and very hurt by what is said about you, or what takes, now that you're in camp. Or at least, I can say I was. Some people even think that you will be gone for life, not thinking that there will be a day that they will have to look you in the eye and speak to you. Out of all of my friends, Dallas was the only one that stood behind me while I went through this ordeal. Don't get me wrong, there may have been one or two that faded in and out, but he had my back. Ironically, Margaret, my ex-wife, really felt that I should be in for life. She made it clear to others what she thought about me. It was clearly obvious that it was easy to talk about someone behind their back. Be prepared, you may experience this and from someone you least expect.

I mentioned that I had a place lined up, right? Wrong! So, I was going to stay with Val and M.D., who I thought were my really good friends. We even had set up the room I would be staying in. I hadn't even been in the camp for 6 to 8 months when I found out that I was not welcome. All of the communication from them was through email through one of their other friends. I had sent an email confirming that I would be coming to stay through a certain period of time, only to receive an unfavorable response of, "absolutely not". I had no Plan B in place and now all of my release paperwork had to be reprocessed. The BOP requests outside contacts and a post release living plan. Thanks a lot, folks! Fortunately, I was able to stay with Dallas for a few months while I could get my act together.

Six months later, I found out that Val had been out drinking with the guys and made the mistake of driving while intoxicated. Consequently, she got caught and was charged with a DUI. How unfortunate. I always knew that Val and M.D. had issues with alcohol, even though I had never drunk with them. I knew them well enough to know that Val had a serious problem. I didn't feel bad for her when I heard the news, in fact, I felt that maybe justice was served, as it should be.

You'll realize at some point, that life has a way of moving on with or without you. You want to do all that you can to continue to be in the game, maintain solid relationships with those that mean the most to you, but understand that people change and you will change. If your family isn't supportive or has sold you out, you have to remember that Plan B needs to be in place before you get here. Prepare yourself for this so that you do not find yourself disappointed. Always have a Plan B in place, focus on yourself and what you want to do once you get out. This is so important for your psychological state, heart, and soul. '

Copouts-Camp

A copout is used to make a staff request. I just sent one in for some more blood pressure medication, as well as to put in an application for a town driver. A town driver is when an inmate needs anything you can drive them to get it. You have a car to drive into town, drop them off at the bus station, or go pick up a pizza for the guards. It's a pretty cool job, that everyone wants. The shady drivers, and there is only one, usually are the ones that are bringing in the contraband for the other inmates, which the big one is cigarettes. Many campers will use a copout to formally ask a question. The biggest question is "When am I going home" or "What status is my release paperwork in"? The staff has a certain amount of time to respond to you, generally within 3 days, which is fair because most of them do not know what's going on and need to find out. There may be one or two that actually have a clue. It's really true that when you work for the government, it does take three people to dig a hole. There is never a straight answer.

On the surface, it appears that the system works. The copouts are also a way for a camper to make a complaint about someone else in the camp.

There are many campers who are unhappy and walk around with a chip on their shoulder. They can do no wrong, they know it all, and will let you know it. Trust me, it won't be long before you know exactly who those people are. They stand out like a sore thumb and you definitely do not want to be one of them.

Creating a copout is pretty simple, so whenever someone wants to tattle on another, it's easy to write a copout. There is this guy at the camp, Eric, who has a permanent medical disability, he's also somewhat blind. He really never says much, but he keeps a stack of copout forms in his locker and is good for a few of them a day. He will write one up for just about anything; noise, illegal food, second hand cigarette smoke, or his bunkmates farts. You'll probably meet an Eric on the inside, just like you probably know a few on the outside. Just like the neighbor who calls the cops on you because your dog has barked one too many times. You know the type.

It's so easy, don't do anything wrong, and follow the rules. If a CO asks you do something, show some respect and just do it. There is no reason to create any waves. Your time is short and there is no reason to upset the apple cart. There is no reason to be a tough guy or to squeal on anyone, not in a place like camp. You may feel the temptation to complaint or be a bitch, but it won't do you any good. While it may allow you to feel good, the campers will not like you. Even though you probably won't get beat up for this, you will create a label for yourself, and it will just make things slow down and you will become more miserable than you already are.

Use the copouts for what they are or they'll become a thorn in your side.

Take a look at the following link, you will see the number of forms that are necessary for anything to get anything accomplished!

https://www.bop.gov/PublicInfo/execute/forms?todo=query

Hands Are Tied- Camp

And yours will be too! Don't expect to get much done while you are in the camp. If you do, you will only set yourself up for disappointment and become very disappointed. You cannot manage anything on the outside from the inside. Don't expect your friends and family to be able to do much for you either. They're busy trying to manage their own affairs. Some campers may even feel that they are among the lost and forgotten. Out of sight, out of mind.

You may have, like I have, interests that need to be protected. Whether it's something you were involved with in your family affairs, a business adventure, or anything, really. Your hands are tied. You want to be able to ask someone to help you with something and they can easily ignore you. What can you do about it? What are you going to do about it? Not a thing, because your hands are tied. Should you give up? No, you really shouldn't. You still want to maintain your status quo until you can get home and deal with all of the things you are involved in. The place in time that you left everything when you went in, will look different from when you come out.

It's really important that you take baby steps with your resolution. There is only so much that you can do when you are down, so to speak. Remember that life is very precious and as long as you have your health, you can solve just about any problem. There is nothing that you cannot accomplish, especially if you're focused and determined. It's almost like a huge puzzle with many small pieces, and they all look alike. You'll find yourself scratching your head and asking what's next? Realistically, all you can do is take it one day at a time, tackling one piece at a time. You can only work on yourself and then work on using all of the clues of the puzzle. Like anything else, it will take some time but don't ever give up because you will find a way to succeed.

That is how it is when you leave the camp for many of us. Some of us have lost everything and know that they must start over and how they're going to accomplish that process. Others, like myself, have a huge pile to work off. Sometimes in life, especially while you're in a camp, you should expect that things may not to go as planned. When we place expectations, we are only setting ourselves up for disappointment.

One of my best buddies, Ed, was going to help me with my children's properties. My POA, Dallas and I took several months to train him, and we did a great job in doing so, if I may say so myself. We were confident that he was on the track for success, but he thought he knew it all and stopped listening to us. He pulled a Thelma and Louise on me and drove that beautiful car off the cliff. This made my time so much more difficult than it needed to be. Dallas had his own life, work, and was already was doing enough for me.

It made things unreasonably difficult for him. Ed dug himself into a big ol' hole before he bailed on me. He went dead silent and stopped communicating all together. At this point, we both wanted to bury him in that hole. How do you fall behind and then blame it on someone else? What a crock of bullshit. This goes to show you, you can't really depend on someone on the outside, when you're on the inside looking out.

Be prepared as the best that you can. You will understand that people will change. It's like riding a wild bull. You ride and ride 'til you can't ride any longer, then you fall off! But that doesn't mean that you throw in the towel. Always work hard to hold onto the very essence that you believe in and you will receive your break. Do yourself a big favor and keep things straight, it will work out for you. You deserve it!

Don't Expect Anything- Camp

I'm sure you've heard that expectations only set you up for disappointment, right?

When you think you have a plan, don't be surprised or disappointment if your plan just doesn't work out the way you expect it to. The best laid out plans by both mice and men, just may not happen when you are indeed the property of the government. It's a sad situation. You're under their complete control. Most people do not know what that looks like or how that feels.

Don't even think for one moment that you are pulling one over on them. You may think that you have put together this master plan and that once executed, you will be on top of that mountain again. Unfortunately, they have another plan in place. The government is a nosey group of people. They have people, who have people, watching people. They scope your every move and they love to watch their own. If you were dealing drugs and it brought you to where you are now today, they're going to continue to keep a very close eye on you. They already know that it was a big source of income for you and there may or not be an alternative income source for you. Don't expect the government to provide you with any form of assistance. They won't. There are really no real programs to let you get a leg up when you get up. You will have to do this on your own. This is especially interesting and difficult since you may now have a felony record. This becomes a huge burden that you will carry with you.

You'll be expected to tow your own line. Don't do anything to cross it when you're either doing your time or when you're finally released. You don't want to be a statistic. You don't want to be violated.

There was this guy, Matt, who had been tagged by the system. Matt's a good guy. He is resilient, and smart. This setback for him is only minor in the scope of the big picture. He'll figure it out. But this is not what you want to happen. So even if you have a good, workable plan, you never know what may happen. Always expect the unexpected. You sure won't think it's fair and it may not be, but don't put yourself out there. The only option you will have, is to work yourself through it. You have to be careful and play by the rules. Stay clear of any trouble. Don't set yourself up for anything. Someone is always watching what you are doing.

Remember to always have eyes on the back of your head at all times… and that the walls have ears.

This is Jail, not Yale:

Don't expect to be treated as though you are at a college campus or that you are at home. It doesn't take much to remind you that this is jail and not Yale. No special treatment here!

Some Days-Camp

Some days, if not most, will never change for you when you're in a camp. Once you are in with a regular routine, one day will roll into the next without much to look forward to, except for the holidays, or maybe a weekend visit. The weeks pretty much come and go.

Your time will go quicker than it actually feels. For some, especially those on the outside, it may be moving at a snail's pace. For you, a month or two to go home is not too far off.

The highlights of you each week will be certain things that you look forward to, as miniscule as they will be. For example, burger and fry day is on Wednesday. Even though the burger is REALLY bad and they don't know how to cook fries. What makes it something to look forward to is because you are relating and eating something that you can relate to the outside with. You may enjoy the eggs on Sunday mornings. There are small eating highs that help pass the time.

You may experience having cravings for certain food that you enjoyed on the outside but that will pass. You can only quickly settle into what they have to offer and hope that you can spice it up whenever you can. Eating tasteless and overcooked food only fills the hunger void. You make do.

No matter how bad a situation is in life, we as humans find a comfort level. We learn not to anticipate more and if you have to, expect less. In essence, you find a level of comfort after some time. You learn to adapt and trust me, you will. What you may have found as abnormal yesterday will become the norm today. Whether it's the bunk you sleep in, the clothes you wear, or the food you eat. If you can get to that level relatively quickly, you will discover that most importantly, the pain is minimal. While you will have an adjustment period, for most of us, that time will be different.

The stepdown guys are the true "bad guys". They're the repeat offenders and they adjust and readjust very quickly, as though it's no big deal. They know that they have one foot in the camp and one foot out the door. They have already been through the hard part, the first go around. This is a piece of cake for most of them. They know the drill, so no big deal. Really, you don't have to know the deal. You just need to know the basic rules that they expect everyone to follow and learn not to talk too much. Nobody cares to hear your opinion, nor do you care to hear theirs. Heh, sometimes I don't care and let it be known anyway! I have always had a knack of bringing substance to a subject and have made a lot of friends. Some of them, I will see on the outside. I will look them up and attempt to help them. It's what I plan to do.

Kevin is going home soon. He is from the country and a move to Roanoke will be a nice change for him and his family. I would like to teach him real estate and find him opportunities for success. He can have the world in the palm of his hands. I'm looking forward to helping him out.

While the fact of the matter is, being in a USP facility, is meant to institutionalize you. You don't want to be, you may even try to fight it. You never want to totally conform to the system. Hold onto a sense of what reality looks like to you and focus on the life you have on the outside. Eventually you will return to it. Don't get those jailhouse blues. You won't have to worry about a cheesy tattoo. They are condoned and could lead you to trouble.

Bud has been at the camp for 16 months. He's started to really enjoy the food. I really don't know how. He's a decent man, around 64 years old, with a really nice family. He's looking at 5 or 6 years to go, and has gotten settled in. I hate this for him. As we are sitting at the lunch table, he's really starting to think that the food is good. I can only think to myself, "No, Bud, the food is not good. It may be okay, but it's far from good food." You can create an illusion of whatever it is that you need to create. It's just a part of the adaptation to life in the camp! But trust me, the food is not good.

My kids asked me what I missed eating the most. Pizza was high on the list. I also missed breakfast from my favorite breakfast place. A bagel could hit the spot right about now. Hey, I could even enjoy a double cheeseburger from McDonalds, at this point. On the other hand, if you don't have something for a while, you get to the point that you really don't miss it much.

I will have to admit, I am looking forward to having quality food very soon. I also look forward to cooking some fine meals, even if I have to eat them by myself. As a day goes by, you will find that the weeks follow pretty quickly. Just before you realize it, you're going to go home!

Activities

There are some activities that you have to be careful of and some that will make you happy to participate in.

Poker-Camp (2)

You will see that they play a lot of poker at the camp. It will come and go, as they may play 4-5 nights a week, and then it may disappear for a few months. The long-timers love to get a whale in the game, as they will act as a pool of sharks and can destroy someone.

Danny, there are several Danny's at the camp, who ideally deserves to be in the camp. From the day he walked into the camp, he promoted himself a God saved Catholic, but has continued to lie to everyone about who his and what he's done. He's a twice convicted felon. He says he has a lot of money, but that's far from the truth. His wife and kids can no longer afford to visit him. Or maybe they really do not want to and are embarrassed by the way he acts. Mr. Big Shot. What he failed to tell anyone is that he has a gambling problem. Yep, he got into the poker game, the sharks consider him a whale and they ganged up on him and ate him up alive. Within a couple of days, Danny was in the game and he was in the hole. In less than a month, he was down $1200.00. I don't know you, but I think that is a lot of money to lose. The poker chips are made from cutting pieces of wood from the fence. They're exactly the same and painted with different colors.

I've heard stories that in some camps, they will take an old deck of cards and cut them into chips.

They play crazy games like Texas Hold'em, Oklahoma, or High Low. They play for nickels, dimes, and quarters, but the pots can grow pretty quickly and you can get down in that hole pretty fast. Danny is really lazy and I do mean REALLY lazy. You can't help but to wonder just how he supports his family, he's that lazy. Last week, he had to take on a job at the commissary at USP in order to pay his debt. They have the highest rate of pay. His bunkie has been overheard saying that he's heard him in his locker getting some commissary items to put in the pot late at night. How crazy is that? They play until 4:00 a.m. This is entirely way too late. One night around 11:00 p.m., I was in the laundry room getting some ice. This is where they play. I was curious so I stuck around and watched them play for a little while.

I saw this crazy glaze come over Danny's eyes. They were sunken in and dark around the edges. He was staring at the cards as if he knew what the pecking order was so that he knew what would take the win. I personally don't think he had any idea what was going on in the game, and the sharks knew it too.

How do you lose that kind of money and remain hungry to want to get into another game? I guess it's like any other junkie. Everyone laughs at him. He has no idea what they are laughing at, that they are laughing at him! Of course, Danny's never admitted to anyone that he's an addict. He's a lousy gambler, he has no money, and he's addicted to it. Gosh, you would think that being sent to a camp would be a wake-up call for someone like Danny, maybe for some. Obviously, Danny did not understand that the punishment of being in camp is enough to get it.

Some people just don't get the message and never will. There are always a few like Danny, always professing his faith but lives his life like a martyr. The time he has in, is not enough. Unfortunately, you cannot count on the BOP to help with your recovery or your resolution. You're on your own!

Softball-Camp

Ah- sports! We all love some sort of sport or two. While you're in camp, you can bet that sports are a great outlet to get involved in. It's a win-win situation for you. You get to have some fun, you get some exercise, it burns away some time, and you get to know people. Now, just take a moment to get a glimpse at what this actually looks like. We're organized, but this is really street ball, like when you're playing with a group of guys in your local park. You don't have to worry about someone coming after you with a baseball bat. There will be a lot of yelling and screaming. I don't yell and scream. I also do my best to pick players who don't participate in that nonsense, either. I am the coach. I pick the players who sign up at the draft. If I pick someone who is a little hotheaded, well I do everything I can to keep him calmed down when we are playing. I don't want a team with that kind of reputation. Tracy, on the other hand, is a screamer. I wonder how he survives on the outside! The first spring seam, I had Tracy on my team. He was suspended for three games for being out too loud and out of control. When it was time to choose teams for the summer team, I did not pick him, just because he's way too loud for me. What a game spoiler! Warren had the pleasure of having him on his team this year, and he seemed to be better at keeping him at bay, than I was. That worked out fine and dandy!

I played softball regularly. Spring, summer, and fall seasons, I could be found organizing for softball, and was most likely on the field. Basketball easily fit in and I looked forward to the draft, a practice or two, as well as the playoffs. The commissary did a great job of keeping it organized. We even had a few referees. During the regular season, there were two games per week, and sometimes you may only play one. While during other times, you may play two games. It made the day go by quickly and you would look forward to the next game that started at 5:15 and would last until 6:30. That is unless someone got the mercy rule. The mercy rule meant that your team was winning by more than 10 runs. This happened from time to time. The games took you into the evening and would usually bring a nice crowd to watch. It was nice having some fans to cheer you on.

I personally played my heart out, doing the best that I could. I never played organized softball before so there was some getting used to the structure of the game. From the high, slow pitch, to the low, fast ball that comes at you when you're playing. I was the pitcher and I have to say, that ball would come at me so hard at times that I was nervous to field it! Sometimes, I would have to step aside, which I hated to do. When that happened, I felt like I was letting the team down. There a few times that I retrieved a hot one, which was great, and I got a lot of high fives when that happened.

The longer I played, the better I became, both in pitching and hitting. I was good for singles, but I could not hit for crap. On an average, I was always near 400, which was pretty good for this old guy! As the games were played, it was really amazing how that helped the days pass by, but it did. The weeks flew by and before we would know it, it was playoff time. The best team got a bye. The two teams on the bottom, which we always seemed to win the best of three to advance. It always seemed like we would put on our dancing shoes and that would do well enough to advance to the playoffs for the championship. What a show we would put on, always knocking out the number one seed. It was a blast, the only real fun that I can honestly say I had while being in the camp.

We had pretty good equipment. The gloves were all good, all nice and broken in. The bats were ok. We could have used a few more, but what we had were still good. We also had a nice supply of balls, but we could have used a few more green ones to replace the ones that they would hit over the fence. When that happened, that was considered a good hit! We were in the mountains of West Virginia, so when a ball was hit over the fence, it was in the woods. Sometimes we would be able to retrieve it, other times we wouldn't. A few weeks ago, one of the guys when after one and saw a huge black bear out there. He was on one side of the fence and the bear was on another. They guy took off running and screaming like a banshee. Was that crazy or what? So if you choose to go on the other side of that fence, you may want to make it quick, just in case you meet up with a bear or some other creature.

The field we played on was actually really good. Warren and Andy made sure of that. The infield was clean, nice dirt, with great running lanes and good bases. The outfield was full of grass that was well mowed.

Both teams, both home and visitors had player benches, and there were even spectator seats on both sides. The only thing that we really lacked was a nice dug out. We had everything else. If you didn't know any better, it was like you were watching a church league on the outside, minus the beer, snacks, and of course women. No women in our camp today, there are just 154 men. We can barely put a team together, but we were close by getting 30 to 35 players, with a couple of substitutes.

Dean was on our team. I wanted him to change, to be liked by the campers. He was not well liked, that's why I chose him. He did nothing to improve his shady image. One of his biggest faults he had was a cackle for a laugh, it reminded me like finger nails scraping down the side of a chalkboard, could not hit or field the ball, so I put him on as a catcher. I wanted him to do well. He thought practice was stupid and that he didn't need to practice. Everyone else on the team though they needed to practice, so we practiced, and as a result, we all played well. We also had a lot of fun at the same time. When it was game time, I wanted to put Dean in the game and did so, even if were wearing headphones, listening to the radio. What a schmuck! Are you kidding me, Dean? We attempted to explain our next move, what the strategy was, and he just didn't get it. He was not listening and it was apparent that he just didn't care. I, at first tried to defend him to the team, but it was useless.

Dean would get up to bat and most likely strike out. There was no effort at all. Even with a 3-1 count, we would yell to take the pitch, that a walk was as good as a hit. He had his stupid headphones on, yes, even when up to bat, and of course he could not hear a thing, nor did he care. He would swing and was called out. He would have the audacity to laugh like a cow that's in heat, joking about it. It was almost like he had placed a bet against us. I was exhausted by the end of the game. He could never throw the ball back to me the same way twice. I had to really read it, almost dive for it from time to time. After 7 innings, I had enough. We put Andy back in to catch. He did a great job. I put Dean in right field and just hoped that nobody would hit the ball out there. That was the best we could have and it sure wasn't much. It was apparent Dean could care less about the team, or even himself. He wasn't much to write home about. He asked me a few times why people didn't seem to like him. I wanted to tell him to read a chapter out of his playbook and hit the road. He was the creation of his own misery.

The next game was only two days away and it was a playoff game. Nobody wanted Sean to play due to his antics and attitude. I invited him onto the team as a sub, and much not to my surprise, he did not even show up. It was typical for the course and quite frankly, we were okay with it. We all played much better and had a great game without him being there. We won! The attitude of our players was the best. Sometimes, you just got to know when to walk and know when to run. Dean couldn't get it.

When you are removed from the world, sometimes, you really are removed and you are stuck with who you have. We are down to 152 campers, as I write this, and that means from 11 to 10 players on our softball team. We did not need Dean, so much for being nice. So long, Dean, we are setting you adrift in the wild blue yonder. Go along your merry way, Dean, just don't look back to see if any of us are there, because we aren't looking for you. I made the mistake of loaning Dean a lot of money to help him and his family out with some storage fees, to retrieve all of his business records and his personal items. While he appeared to be grateful, it did not change his attitude. He was still the same person that nobody could seem to like. I liked him enough to help him, but I did not see the wolf in the sheep's attire, until it was too late. I'll never step up to plate to help him out again, at least not in this life time.

Come to find out, he's gone! Well, that's what I found out when he didn't show up for the game. He quit. What a joke, there is no way to have a great deal of respect or lack therefore of, for that, but that's the nature of the beast in a place like this. Thank Goodness, this dude, Brandon came back, and signed up the next day to play. We are back in the saddle, with a full line up, which is great for us. We are in the middle of the playoffs, so let's see how this pans out!

Basketball is not my sport. What is nice is that they have some really nice courts to play on. They have a concrete court, which is a half-court, and difficult to play on, but it's okay. If you have ever been to your local park, that's about what you may find there, as well as at the camp. Just like softball, it's just like streetball, more than anything else. The guys who play, play hard, almost too hard for a guy like me. Smylez is the best player at our camp. He's like a one-man wrecking machine. He can get it done and was tough for anyone to play against him. Count on someone at your camp who is as good, and will give the rest of the camp a lesson.

There is a lot of arguing, more than what normally would take place, which can be sort of fun to observe. One thing is for sure, you don't want to get caught up in the middle of those arguments. The basketball games attract a nice size crowd and are worthy of a good watch. Too bad they don't sell hotdogs and cold beer. If they did, it would be an additional crowd pleaser and a great way to make some money.

Sports are a good way to chase away your time. They will keep you busy. They give you something to look forward to. Enjoy this while you can, because there really are not many other activities to get involved in.

The Great Release

Going Home

298 days to go! That's about 43 weeks and yes, we are keeping track. John's a buddy of mine and if it all goes well for him, he may get a halfway house and be eligible sometime after Christmas. If it goes badly, then we are looking at June departures.

Here's a valuable piece of information. Just because it's written in the manual, doesn't necessarily make it true. What you read and what you actually witness about going home, just doesn't add up. It's all on your case worker and what they actually do.

One thing will hit you in the face while you are in USP or a camp. How are you going to survive on the outside? Some inmates may have lost everything, any assets, homes, businesses, and even worse, friends and family. The government's taken every bit of it from you. They love getting their hands on your "stuff"; property, money, vehicles, and whatever else they find of value.

Here you are, paying off your debt to society, behind a wall. You work a lousy job making .25 cents per hour, which may cover a few phone calls during any given month. Maybe you will have a place to stay when you get out, but with no car, no job, money or phone. There is nothing to jumpstart your life. This will most likely deflate you. Your mindset must be right so that you can figure out your next step. Are you a survivalist or are you going to let this defeat you to the point that you find yourself coming right back?

Jimmer went home this week. He had a good wife and family waiting for him. It's amazing that he was finally able to leave. He was 38 days from his release date. Jimmer was an exceptional athlete. Whatever he played, he played hard and was very competitive. What was great was that he spent maybe a little over 100 days in the 18 months that he was here. Jimmer felt his greatest punishment was not to spend any money to live off of in the USP. This was his way to pay his price for getting into trouble. He just did not go to the commissary. He thrived on using other people's old sneakers. He would use the free hygiene products, such as tooth paste, etc. He was such a cheapie, but someone could really learn to survive on nothing by watching Jimmer. His sense of humor matched his habits. They fit his bill perfectly. So, if you're tight on money and cannot get it from home, you can make it through your camp experience without too much difficulty.

Or you can be like Danny. He never ceases to amaze me. Ever since the moment he walked into the camp, he has lied about everything. He's a twice convicted felon and now here for food stamp fraud that he committed in party stores. He claims he owns the store. This is a blatant lie. He was barely a manager. His said his food stamp crime was only $375.00, when in fact it was near $140,000.00. All he ever did consistently was lie at the camp. He had a job in the garage with me and during the 120 hours per month, he maybe worked 10 to 15 of them. What's even worse, is that he was proud of that! There is no re-entry into your life if you don't take steps to improve yourself. This is the place to do it. I am not sure the BOP recognizes it. If Danny can't hold a silly job in the camp, how is he going to be responsible when gets out?

Last month, during the lockdown at the Pen, he went with me to work. Well, he went with me to so called work with me. Danny did nothing but stand around because he's lazy and didn't WANT to work. He stood around with his buddy, Black, and watched me do all of the work. Then he had the audacity to claim he did all of the work. This flew all over me and I let him know it. So, in order to retaliate, he went to main cafeteria and told the campers that were there that I said racial slurs about them. Another lie created by Danny. I don't buy into racial slurs, never have, and never will. I was hot under the collar, but I didn't say a word to Danny. I didn't want to get in the middle of another Danny situation. You don't want to get in the middle of other people's situations. It's not worth the time, energy or aggravation. I just cut off communication with Danny. He knew he did wrong. He created some tension between me and some of the black campers he lied to. I diffused this quickly through some of the other campers. It was the best thing I could do by going in through the back door, of which I did.

On top of all of it, Danny was gambling every night and continued to lose. Today he owes many campers all kinds of money.

You see when you go away, you can be anyone you want to be, and get anyone to believe anything you say. Danny comes across as a successful entrepreneur, as an owner of all of these party stores. He created an illusion that he was very wealthy. A tough guy, he is not. Some people are laughing at him, calling him a town fool. There is no money, there is no business, not even a job. He's nothing but a lazy bum. That's the real Danny! The jokesters in the camp refer to him as the matador, but he's a loser. He continues to gamble, with the mindset that he will earn all of his money back. He's the only white guy in the high-stakes games, and the other players want a piece of him. The other day, the winners all had Danny in a room, having a chat. Guess what that's all about!? I wonder if it were worth their time and effort, my guess is not!

So, take note. It's probably not advisable to gamble, no matter where you are, whether it's a camp or a big house. There are a lot of folks that gamble, and find it as a means of survival. They take it very seriously. If you bet or borrow, you must make sure that you pay it back, and quickly. There are also campers that will buy cigarettes on the black market. If you do this, make sure that you are the first to pay the person you've bought them from. These activities are not good habits to form while you are in a camp. It does not help your re-entry to society plan. Your issues and problems today will follow you tomorrow. Do not kid yourself. Nothing goes away.

I work with Rick, who is from Pittsburg. I have become friends with his son Jeffrey. Jeffrey is a special needs fellow. Rick only has a year. What is cool about Rick is that he was an NFL referee back in the early days and was very well respected. As a kid, Rick would take the train to the NFL games with his dad. Rick remembers meeting Vince Lombardi, Bart Starr, and Johnny Uriates, to name a few. Rick is proud of his son Jeffrey and their pillars of success. Rick can't wait to get home, by the way. He has 16 season tickets to the Pittsburgh Steelers games, burning an imaginary hole in his pocket. That will be so much fun…he's counting down the days.

Below you will find a poem written by an inmate that I never met. It's a clearly, well written poem that summarizes what it's like for some of us when we are anticipating going home.

End Of A Journey
© **Ken Budden**
Published: April 2011

The end of your journey is now in sight,
And from the darkness you can now see light,
I know it's been tough, but I'm hoping you know,
From that hard bitter lesson, "You reap what you sow".
I wrote a letter each week all through the years,
To try and dispel your earlier fears,
That friends would forget you, never want you again,
And I know it happened…wish I could spare you the pain.
For those who forsook you, give them no thought,
They were never true friends and never your sort,
Start a new life, you've gone from "boy to a man,"
And you know I will help you as much as I can.
But you're coming home stronger and wiser I feel,
All your heartaches and heartbreaks will eventually heal,
You have a young son who will need you each day,
And I know you will love him in the best possible way.
It's going to be hard, I'll not lie to you,
But manners and humility will see you through,
Do not be afraid to ask for advice,
That's what I'm here for and "cheap at the price."
Temptations will come, but it's time to be strong,
Just remember the first time and what you did wrong,
Do you really want to be locked up again?
And put friends and loved ones through more terrible pain?

I am not so religious as I really should be,
I only pray in an emergency,
But He'll answer my prayers and those of my friend,
And see your life through to a fruitful end.
Just want you to know, Son, I will always be here,
I will never for sake you, I love you so dear,
One day I will be gone, but these words will remain,
And if ever in doubt please read them again.

Love, Dad. Xxxx [18]

39 and Counting- Camp

Once you get to under a year, it's like a great sigh of relief. You may think that it is an eternity. You have completed most of your time, and you're almost out the door. You've paid your dues and you are ready to meet freedom.

John and I are counting down together. He's leaving a week or so before I am. He has it marked on several calendars, one at work, one at this bunk, next to the pictures of his teenage daughters. This has been a constant reminder of what the price he has paid, as well as the sacrifices his family has made. It's been a difficult road for him and his family. He can't wait to get back home and get his life back on track. I can't blame him because I am on board with that, as well. It's a little nerve wracking now that it's only 39 weeks and counting. It seems now, as it has been in the past, that the days are now sometimes long, and the weeks fast. Whether it's one year or 5 or more, time actually flies by! You're isolated from the world except for the TV, news print, or maybe the visits from your family.

Wouldn't it be nice to be able to go to your favorite restaurant for a good meal? I know many of us would like that!

The week goes by as quick, as we have stayed busy during the time at the camp. By this time, little things will most likely start to bother you. You're becoming seasoned, so to speak! The cam has 7,090 turned over and by the time you leave in 39 weeks, there will be an additional 2,090. 1,090 of those

---

[18] https://www.familyfriendpoems.com/poem/to-my-son-coming-home-from-prison

at the camp are long-timers. Almost scary, 6 to 8 year and 10-year sentences. I can't even imagine how difficult that would be, for not only myself, but for my family, as well. Unless you've committed murder or some other heinous crime, it just seems like such a waste of money, let alone any type of consideration for human life. No wonder the government's budget is so out of balance and out of proportion. Here's a thought, they sure know how to make a mess but they really have a difficult time cleaning it up. It's tough for them for whatever reason. Okay, I'm going to get a little political. How about they balance the budget and hold law makers fiscally responsible. It's pretty simple!

Every Wednesday, I walk across the parking lot to where John works, for the ceremonial pulling down of the calendar page of the week that we just passed. This week, Wednesday is hamburger day, we will pull down week number 39, woot! Woot! We are on week number 38. Just remember, the small milestones will help you. It's September 2012, Labor Day's coming up, Halloween is in 60 days or 8 weeks, which drops us down to 30 weeks remaining. Then Thanksgiving is 90 days out, which puts us to 27 weeks. Don't forget, I keep telling you that time will fly by. You can catch your favorite college or pro football team as this helps pass the time too. There are baseball playoffs, hockey may start up, or even tune in to some round ball. While I'm not trying to advocate TV, all of the new seasons start up shortly after Labor Day. This helps pass the evenings by.

Right after Halloween, you will start seeing the Christmas ads pop up! Yes, Christmas is only 120 days away or just 16 weeks, and we will almost have just 20 weeks to go by, and then it's the first of the year, which is unseeming right around the corner. Everyone will start talking about the crappy steak dinner that they will serve us for New Years and who their prediction will be for the Superbowl. That's 5 weeks away. It's upon you for the annual Superbowl party. It's not one like you will have at home, but it's as close as it gets. That's right, we have 16 weeks and counting to go. At this point, you hope to have had all your paperwork squared away, signatures and all. Did you get your paperwork signed with your case-manager? I hope you have a good case-manager. Be sure that all of your house at home is in order, no guns, or hard-wired phone. Your talk revolves around your release. You can't help but to start to get really excited about your upcoming release. Just keep it simple and you will be fine.

The time is now really getting shorter and shorter. The weeks are clipping by. The cold weather is all but gone, and Easter is around the corner. That's really the best big holiday. There is that 3-day holiday weekend, along with Memorial Day, another 3-day weekend. Then you'll be done with that nonsense. You're just below 10 weeks, and that huge amount of time you had is suddenly reduced to nothing. You're almost there, on the outside looking in!!

You may work a little bit more, maybe do get some workouts in, so you look good when you go home. Do you know if you're taking a bus, or is someone picking you up? I know that John and I will have someone at the front door at 7:30 sharp. Whoever is ready to pick us up, you can't be here prior to 7:30. Some people don't have any choice and have to depend on a bus. Who wants to take their time and go home on a bus? It leaves in the late afternoon. Not me, I will ready to leave here at 7:30, I'm not sticking around until 1:00 p.m. No way! I can't imagine enduring any more discomfort, hanging around for any more time than I have to. By 1:00 p.m., who knows you may have already have gotten a quickie in or something good to eat. You have to get outside, get a fresh change of clothes, and take a deep breath filled with freedom. It's long overdue, this is your day, and it's time to get out of here.

I can tell you that eating lunch during my time here at the camp, with the same people, has been an experience within itself. Some people have really gotten to enjoy the garbage that they serve. It's the cheapest food available on the planet. There is little to no imagination put into the menu that some overpaid brainiac put together. That's the first person that needs to go, fire the head of nutrition! It sure would save the feds a lot of money. How is it that the government promotes health and wellness to its citizens and cannot follow their own rules? I can't help to laugh at how overweight and unhealthy the people are that work for the BOP. Another step towards institutionalizing the people in any form or fashion they possibly can. They start with the schools, nursing homes, and end up in the prisons. Let's get on board the train, people!

During many of my lunches, I had the opportunity to sit next to Bud, who was from Virginia, as well. Bud kind of grew on me after a while. He figured out his routine to pass his days. He dove into his Bible and did a lot of writing. There was not a lot of conversation around his readings. He fulfilled his purpose, which was perfect for him. I always enjoyed our short conversations about current events. We seemed to be on the same page about many of the topics we would discuss. Occasionally, someone with a way out there, left idea would try to start an argument, I would excuse myself, and make my way to the dish room. I was not interested in any argumentative conversations with anyone, especially Tony or Dean, who just were not practical in any way.

Anyway, Bud is 64 years old and just started his 8-year sentence. I guess he's got maybe 6 years to go. He will be 70 years old when he gets out. To me, that's a lifetime. He's a devoted family man and he loves his wife. It's such a sweet scene, almost perfect when everyone shows up to visit and support him. He has just started his long journey. I pray that he will receive an early release so he can be with his family. He thinks that he that may happen for him, he's almost banking on it. I'm not sure that's how it works. There are a lot of people in camp that think that a miracle is right around the corner and that they will be going home.

Unfortunately, the government has their own set of rules, once they've got their hooks into you, they don't let you go too easily. It's terrible but it is what it is. That's why I have worried about Bud, he will probably have to all of his time alone. Most of the few people he's friendly with now, will have gone.

Here are some links to some fascinating stories about a few people in the know that have spent time with the BOP. Enjoy!

- https://www.yahoo.com/entertainment/tim-allen-recalls-serving-time-prison-cocaine-charges-201655802.html
- https://www.grunge.com/193922/the-truth-behind-merle-haggards-time-in-prison/
- https://www.mashed.com/240834/the-truth-about-martha-stewarts-time-in-prison/

Time Served- Camp

As the days turn into weeks, the weeks into months, you will accumulate "time served". This is time that you have already done, something you will never have to do again. It's a great feeling to look back at your time served and take reference that you have served some serious time. What is better than that is to look ahead and be able to count the days, the weeks, and the months.

If you have some time to serve, it's going to be a little harder in the beginning and there is no way around it. Let's just say they hand you 10 years and you have served 14 months. It may seem like it's going to drag on forever. I have a few friends in the camp with that dilemma. They walk around looking a little bewildered from time to time. There are some blue-collar guys who are somewhat still in denial. Most of them continue to try to work their cases either on an appeal level, a 2255, or even a Rule 35. They look for any possible angle they can to get themselves out early. They're not leaving next week but they want out as soon as possible.

My friend Freddy is on of six people who got a lot of time for RICO election fraud and a few other infractions. His friends got over 20 years each, and in some cases, it was life sentence they were looking at. They were sure to be leaving the camp in a casket. They say that the older we get, the smarter we are. Well, I guess in some cases, this is true. Maybe some people continue to play with fire like they did when they were younger, thinking that they won't get burned. Then they get burned, they get caught and their lives go to hell in a hand basket pretty quickly. I have gained respect for the system. Some of Freddy's friends or codefendants are in their 70's, some of them are even ill. Short of killing someone, how much time should someone really get? It's a tough question to really answer.

Freddy's family has been contacted by many movie production companies, like HBO, and national magazines and newspapers, like the Washington Post. They want to buy his story. They're requesting publishing and movie rights. It would be a perfect case for a movie. That doesn't do Freddy much good, since he has 12 years to serve and has only served 3. His case is under an appeal. Already, many of the charges against have been dropped. Their case is falling by the wayside. I bet between all of those who were involved, they are all working in tandem to win. One wins then they all win, so that is good. Over 200, 000 on legal fees. They have legal teams all over the country that are very good and doing a great job to help.

The prosecuting feds have done all that they can to dodge all of the bullets that are coming their way. They ask for extension after extension, hoping the case will go away. It's not going away. Freddy and his codefendants are determined, but what tears you apart is not seeing your son or daughter who may be having a baby. You aren't able to care for your aging parents, or have control over the sale of your personal items. It's not quite right. I talk to Freddy and we commiserate over the fact that Freddy should be released along with his codefendants, while the government takes their good old time that they need until all of the appeals are exhausted. Sounds like common sense to me. Logical too, but we all know there is no common sense or logic when it comes the federal government.

So, you may spend a lot of time working hard, hoping and praying that you will get some sort of relief, at some point. Sitting in a camp, knowing that you have all of those years to serve, and know that there will not be much left of your life when you get out, is a hard pill to swallow. In the back of your mind, you are thinking about all those states where inmates are being released from prisons for committing some hard crimes, serving little to no time at all. Here you are, shaking your head, wondering how you're going to deal with any more than what you've already served. It's a tough road to travel.

Freddy's case is becoming a high-profile case, that someday may become a movie, but certainly won't pay him a high enough price like he had to pay with his codefendants.

Another friend of mine, Bud, I've mentioned him before. He's a family man from Richmond. He's done a little over a year and has an 8-year sentence. At this point, he has about 6 years to go. He pretty much stays to himself, in an effort to pass his time. He has a loving family like Freddy and also gets a lot of visits. The visits connect with home, enables you to have hope, and keeps you grounded. You need hope. You've got to have it. Don't ever give up your dreams. The time you're in the camp, is only a minor setback in the big picture of your life. It's a hurdle you have to work through.

What I found out early on, is that with the lack of connection with the outside, you find yourself almost hopeless. You cannot get anything done. Some people who respect for will attempt to help you, but may not really want to do anything. I have had a lot of things to do on the outside. More than most, I would say. Just so I would not miss a beat, I was personally managing my children's property, as well as just maintaining as many of the things I possibly could. As my oldest son Roland told me, "Dad, it's amazing what you can get done. Most people cannot multi-task like you can. You always expect them to operate at your level, but most people cannot. So, you become disappointed in them. But truly, they are doing the best that they probably can. Try to give them a break". Maybe in the end, it all works out for the best, but you never know until you are there. Traveling the path is surely very frustrating. You will wonder when it's going to be enough. I get it. Whatever the message is for the crime I've committed, I get it. You could have sent me home a long time ago and I would have still gotten the point. So really, tell me, what is the point? Is it to show me your power? Or is it your ability to put a band-aid on a broken system? A system that is unjust and has a terrible habit of over punishing people at a horrendous cost. You will spend many hours thinking how wrong it really is.

Bud spends most of his days working on his religious studies. I never knew that someone could spend so much time on them, but he does. I am sure that he has retained his knowledge. In here, you don't, I mean you won't want to talk to many campers about your religious opinions. They are way too judgmental and there is no need to put yourself out there. I don't know how many people are truly versed on the facts. Many will have skimmed the surface and talk about what they think that they know. Right or wrong, they will argue very hard for what they believe in.

What doesn't matter is the conversation, because if they believe it then surely, they are entitled to their beliefs. Who are you to challenges someone else's beliefs? You cannot do that and should not do that. It's not even worth opening up the door to even have that discussion. Talk about other things, anything else. Stick with subjects that just don't make a difference, ones that nobody will really care about. Worthless, meaningless topics that you can have with just about anyone. It's best for your sanity if you handle it that way.

Bud started a bible study, which was a great idea. The bible study attracted many people, an average of 15, about 10% of the camp. It was easy to feel comfortable with the people who were there. Those people had a common purpose and goals. This was a safe environment to discuss your thoughts and promote an agenda, that is if you have one. Not to say that an agenda could give yourself some peace, or bring a good solid dialogue about a worth subject to those who wanted to participate. Nobody was being forced to go or speak up.

Bud worked tirelessly on the subject matter and each week, he put on a terrific class. He was well prepared. The sermons were well organized. He did not want it to be a free-for-all and it was not. The structure allowed for a good lesson plan, followed up by questions and conversations. He was always pleased with the way it all turned out. Everyone who went received a price benefit for going. This was a wonderful opportunity that Bud put together.

This was a great way of passing a lot of time for Bud. He keeps on telling me how many hours it takes him to prepare and how fulfilled he is after the class. Good for him. Bud has spent a great deal of time trying to heal personally, which I worry about. He is making progress, but being here has taken a toll on him, and it's not good for him, as it's not for many of us. He's able to get some peace by helping others and this is great for him. I just hope he will continue sharing his knowledge and thoughts with others.

We all work through each day, everyone doing their time in a different way. We all just want to put one more day behind us and get one day closer to going home. Sounds reasonable to me!

After a while you'll be at a point where you think to yourself, what do I do next?

Nothing to Do- Camp

Some days, you may feel like you've hit a brick wall. Ball season may be over with, the weather may have turned, work is just work, playing cards gets old, and so do board games. There may only so much conversation to be had. You really don't know what you're supposed to be doing.

Don't expect to be entertained with you come to the camp. There is no entertainment director that you may find on the cruise that you're on. Nobody is going to take an extra step to make you feel comfortable, or keep you busy.

Have you found yourself bored today? Totally out of your mind, bored? Maybe the snow day has got you tied down to your house. You're snowed in, so what's the plan to keep yourself busy. You can only get in so many small projects, may watch some TV, do a little reading, eat a little lunch, and have a few snacks. Maybe your day will go by and you will feel good about what you were able to accomplish. That's perfect! Right?

Now, can you do that every day for a year or more? How busy can you keep yourself? Here's the difference between a snow day on the outside and on the inside. You're restricted to the space that you live in, as well as not having access to the things that you may want or need. Okay, as you can see that's a challenge. Be prepared, there may be times that you are bored stiff. Anything that you can do to eliminate the boredom, is a big plus. Working, working out, reading, sleeping, writing, watching TV, and sleeping some more. There are many simple things that you can do to pass the time. I would not wait until the sense of boredom strikes, jump right in there, and tackle your time. If you find that something is not fulfilling that itch, then try something else until you hit that groove. You want to keep your mind active. That really helps to keep me connected. It was also something that I did when I was on the outside. There is always something in the bag that will grab your attention.

So, if you're not use to being bored, get ready, because you will definitely find yourself in that position. Do a few things in preparation, before you come into the camp. Order a newspaper, magazines, or books that you will want to read. Get some pens, paper, and a journal. Write about your thoughts, feelings, and experiences. Reach out to your family by writing them letters. Develop a workout plan. Work on your re-entry plans. Do whatever it is possible that you can to from keeping the boredom from driving you nuts. Trust me on this!

Boots to the Ground- Camp

I had only heard this term in the military. With the recent wars in the Middle East, along with many civilians discussing the air and land attacks. Boots to the ground refers to our foot soldiers having their boots literally on the ground, ready for action.

I hope that you are never in this type of situation, but if you are ever in a confrontation you want to have your boots on. I have seen where something becomes a reality, an argument starts to escalate, one of the guys involved has his boots on. The other did not. He gets up, leaves, goes to his bunk, and puts his boots on.

When you first see this, I must admit, it's quite strange. I would think a fight is a fight, boots or not. I guess having your boots on provides you with stability on the ground. If you are a kicker, it gives you a little more to your kick.

Don't put yourself in a bad situation and you won't have to worry about it. If someone goes to put their boots on, well, walk the other way. I have enjoyed the drama associated with it all. You know, a good fight every now and then, is actually pretty healthy.

Drama-Camp

Drama, it may be the only B.S. you will have to deal with today. If nothing else, it's entertaining and will keep you going. There is enough idle conversation to keep you busy throughout your day. Thankfully, nobody talks politics or what's happening on the inside because they either don't have a clue or they really don't care. The days are filled with conversations about when somebody is going home. This is what the focus is on! Everyone continually tries to figure out their exact date to depart. You see, even if your paperwork is complete, your home release date is indicated, but that doesn't mean it's correct. You will hear other inmates discussing how their case manager is a piece of shit, that he's not sent in your paperwork, or he's quite behind. You question why your case manager can get away with spending hours playing solitaire and your paperwork is sitting on his desk. What a joke.

My buddy Chris was supposed to go home on a Monday. He's a good guy, he actually went to the same high school that I did in Wayne, New Jersey. Four days before he was supposed to leave, it was discovered that he was going to go home to house confinement and that his probation officer had yet to receive his paperwork. This was ridiculously crazy because Chris had been at the camp for three years. You would have thought at sometime during those three years, the process would have been completed. Another example of a broken governmental system. You will see quickly how poorly it is managed and that you are a victim of it, as well.

What is upsetting, is how much money the government profits, how much government employees make and the benefits they received despite the fact that are low producers. One CO that does electrical work at the camp told me that it just doesn't pay to work hard because the harder you work, the more they expect, and the less appreciation you will receive. It's almost like you are encouraged to go backwards and most typically do. I can only think that this is just the system. No wonder there is a lot of time wasted talking about how crazy the entire system is. You will hear the same stories over and over again until you are numb from listening, or blue in the face from talking.

Another thing that creates drama in the camp is cutting in the lunch line. First of all, there is no reason to do it, the food isn't going anywhere, and it's clearly not good enough to fight to get to it. You're going to eat to fill the void. When someone cuts in line it shows a lack of respect. Some inmates make a big deal over this, instead, just don't let it happen. You can say something very casually and they will back off.

Then there is the noise. Everyone is constantly complaining about the noise. The biggest problem occurs at night after the 9 p.m. count. It's usually the younger fellows that don't want to work and those who get away with sleeping late. There are so many noises and at different pitches and levels. So many noises you are not accustomed to. It will take sometime to adjust to them. I suggest if you are moving bunks, that you check out the noise levels first. In the meantime, don't create any additional drama over it.

Fight-Camp

Do not under any circumstance put yourself in a situation that you are a part of a fight. There may be times when you will find yourself so frustrated that you will want to smack someone upside the head. Allow that feeling to pass. Trust me, it will be a disaster if you allow that to overcome you. Most camps have a zero-tolerance policy for fighting. Pushing and shoving can be considered as instigating a fight. Always bite your tongue, control yourself, and move on, even if it creates a pit in your stomach.

It is much easier to get involved in an altercation in the TV room or in the yard. Just because you've been there, have put in some time, it doesn't give you permission to feel like you own the TV or the basketball court. Don't have any conversations that will open the doors for trouble. You will be the bigger person if you just walk away from these situations.

I worked with a guy for over a year. His name was Ray, who was a good guy with some intelligence. He was a family man. He had filed a 2255, with the hope of receiving some relief on his 8-year sentence. Last week he was in the TV room, just like any other night for the past several months. A conversation between Ray and Q took place. Q is another good guy, he's quiet, respectful, and a step-down guy. There were never any issues between these two fellows. Unfortunately, they got into a heated verbal match over something silly. Ray ended up leaving the TV room and went to his bunk to put his boots on. I couldn't believe it. Ray was much smarter than this. He allowed his emotions and pride get to the best of him. It's so much better when you swallow your pride and walk away. Well, Q followed Ray to his bunk and jumped him. Q was armed with a lock in a sock and cut Ray's forehead, above his eye. He ended up with a blackeye. You can joke about having a lock in a sock, but it's not advisable in camp. Really, you don't need to protect yourself. It's really not necessary unless you like to invite trouble.

Ray, who is 275 pounds, a former football player for the Chicago Bears, quickly got up and threw Q to the ground. Q is 225 pounds of solid muscle, so he's quite strong. They got into it pretty quickly. Ray had his arm against Q's neck and was choking him. Q bit his arm. Holy shit! Finally, someone came in and broke it up and the bunk area was cleaned up. It did not take long for the two of them to make peace. They both thought it was all over with, and really it should have been. To my surprise, there were over 15 cop outs in that fight. A counselor was called in to investigate. We were all perplexed. Ray and Q both thought that it was a done deal.

Ray come to work, nursing his cut, and was talking about his 2255 and what a good deal this was going to be. Unfortunately, it did not take long before Ray was summoned to the USP and questioned again. When he came back, he still assumed it was a closed case. It wasn't an hour later that they summoned him again. This time, he was thrown into the hole. Nobody knew what was going on. The next day the USP summoned Q and he was taken to the hole, as well. Q's personal belongings were packed up. He wasn't returning. Everyone was feeling the pain from this ordeal. They both were in the hole on our campus at the USP. It was hard to say what was going to happen. Some people were even speculating that they might get back into the camp. Some of us wanted that to happen except for those who wrote the cop outs.

Take note that there are some campers that think they are better than everyone else. They can say and do what they want at will. It's pretty absurd but it is how it is on the inside and on the outside.

When we first heard that Q was not coming back, we could see that was a possibility. Afterall, he attacked Ray. Then we heard that Ray would be returning and we were okay with him returning. I know I wanted him to come back. Two days later, on a Sunday night, Ray's items were packed up. I had heard from Kevin, who was on laundry distribution, that the CO said Ray was not coming back.

So, as you can see, you really have to feel for this situation. While you may not like it, you have to be able to accept it and move on. It did not take but a day before two bottom bunks were filled. Filled quickly, they were. A dead man is forgotten very quickly in camp.

Surprise- Camp

So, be prepared, just like on the outside, you will get many surprises while you are at the camp. Remember when you were young and you spent a week at wilderness camp with kids you hardly knew? It probably did not bother you much if they acted the way they did. Some of them, maybe pretty strange. As you know, after time, a year or two with the same people, over and over again, you can count on things, anything, will grate on your nerves. You have to show your strength and keep your composure in order to get by. You're not going anywhere. You're always best just not saying anything. Don't ask any questions, either.

One morning, I was going to the garage job on the bus, and Steve and Red were with me. Steve and I were joking around like we always do, having a few laughs before he dropped me off. Red, who is from Virginia, like I am, was a recovering drug addict who doesn't ever say much. He is really pretty strange. It's either his personality or the vast amounts of drugs he's taken over the years. In the six months he's been at the camp, we've been good. Until this particular Friday when I was asking him some questions of no value. I asked him what they were working on, trying to strike up a conversation, maybe for entertainment purposes. Out of the blue, Red snaps at me and says, "Man, you ask a lot of questions". Ok, I have to take a step back and I say, "Hey, dude, I said I wouldn't ask you any more questions, if you feel like I'm bothering you". He really isn't very intelligent, and drugs will do that to you.

Why even try to be nice to anyone? I spent some time after that encounter scratching my head and wonder where did he think he was? I mean, did he forget where he was and the type of people he was dealing with? That's not to say that church going people wouldn't respond the same way, but let's face it most of these people in the camp didn't get here by going to church every week. They sure make a lot of mistakes, they knew the risks, and took a shot.

So, here we have a guy by the name of Red, who has a bad attitude, and thinks that I ask too many questions. Do I care? Well, sure I care. Should I care? No, I shouldn't care at all, but I do. Maybe I am one of the few in the camp that has a kindred and caring spirit. It's easy for a duck to let water roll down his back, maybe not quite so easy for you or someone else. You may want to toughen up your skin a little bit. I am sure that when you go home, there will be some people that will notice some changes in you. This may be one of those changes.

Always consider your source. I have met many people in camp and have spent some time wondering how someone can do some of the amounts of time some of these guys are doing. Five, seven, and even ten years. It's really hard to wrap your head around that amount of time. You have to have your head right when you come into camp. Truly do your best to mind your own business. You do not want to get yourself involved in anyone else's business at all. You quickly find a way to do your own time so that you are comfortable and stay out of everyone's way.

After a few months, you will have settled in a bit, and you sure will find little things that people may do that will annoy you. I'd like to share some of what annoys me. Snoring, a filthy bunkmate, the guy that's walking to the showers with his shirt off, rattling ice in a drink container, and someone that doesn't hold back when farting in public. Some people have some disgusting habits. Some people's laughs get on my nerves, just like those who eat while they're talking, or the guy that's always asking you for something. Then there are those who are a nosey busybody, or those who think they should look up your case. Oh, and there's a guy named Johnson in here, he never showers, not ever. We've told him he stinks badly, and all he does is smile. How disrespectful. You don't want to get involved, you just find a good area to bunk in and do your own thing.

As time goes on, you will have a few friends and a few enemies. People will talk and some will talk about you. Just don't pay any attention to them. Be the bigger person, in any and all situations. Unlike me, don't allow this stuff to get the best of you. Sometimes I do okay but there are times when I do not. I usually try to sit tight for a few days, bite my tongue and not say much, even if it does bother me. I have tried to turn the other cheek and for the most part, it has worked. Keep in mind that the level things may bother you today, may be minimal tomorrow. Just grin and bear it. Most people don't realize what they're doing. They really do think that farting in public is just fine, or eating and talking at the same time are acceptable. You never want to be like them, that's the bottom line. Don't make fun of anyone. Certainly, don't correct them. As of tomorrow, it sure won't even be on your list of priorities. You may not even think about for a few weeks.

Keep an open mind, expect surprises, and just go with the flow. If it becomes unmanageable, then take the high road, and just walk away.

Small Talk- Camp

You should expect that when you are housed with the same people day in and day out, you may get into some lengthy conversations with some people. It may be good to be able to talk with someone who you can connect with. Having a connection with the right person and being able to trust them, is important. People will change in any environment that they are in. You may think that you know someone, but remember that you really don't. Truthfully, who do you really know? Really, do you even care? You are just passing through.

Small talk is fine and dandy, but anything beyond that, you may want to keep yourself guarded. There may be no reason to go beyond that. In the time that I was at the camp, I did not have too many in depth conversations with too many people about me or what I had on my mind. There was no need. Personally, I knew that I could not trust too many people at the camp. Why would I, when I obviously couldn't trust too many people on the outside. It's really no different.

I noticed that most people were really more interested in themselves than anyone else. Their story was the most important thing in the world, their stories mostly are about their case, and the injustice that was served to them.

You will need to develop good listening skills. Don't interrupt, let them go on and on. If you can and want to interject, you may be able to, but don't count on it. This is one of those times that you don't want to open your closet door. It's closed and it's full of baggage that you want to leave behind closed doors. Leave it closed and you'll be better off. Talk spreads like wild fire in here, you don't want your story out there.

I trusted my bunkmate, Tony. He was respectful, you won't be able to say that about too many people. Be cautious with what you say to others, how much information you provide about yourself to anyone. There is really no reason to open your heart to anyone. Another one of those things to avoid. In the time that I spent in the camp, nobody knew me. They saw me as someone that they thought that they knew, but they had no idea, and really, I didn't care much to share anything with them. There was no need.

Some people at the camp are like an open book. They just let the flow of information about themselves come out. Maybe it was some sort of release for them, an opportunity to shed some long-carried baggage, a chance to get rid of it. Maybe they felt better afterwards.

Stick to the small talk. Let everyone else do their own talking, just listen and take it all in. It's the best thing you can do for yourself. Sometimes, it's best just to stand back and be the observer.

26 Weeks

I had my last visit with my children, or at least I told them it was their last visit. I had not received too many visits over the 21 months that I was at the camp. In the beginning, it was very hard because I knew that other people were receiving visits. Especially those that lived around you would get the call to go to the visiting room. Some guys had visits every week, some occasionally, then others that never had anyone come to see them.

After the initial shock of being at the camp, you do settle in, but you will also settle into some boring and lonely weekends. As time goes by, even though you miss your family, it becomes easier to handle. Traveling for some can become very expensive. Many of the camper's families came great distances to visit. Some had to make lodging accommodations, others did not. There are all of the extras, as well, such as food.

When you get a visit, it will lift your spirits. It makes you feel loved, cared for, and supportive. You'll feel better, it will keep you somewhat sane, and maybe even motivated for the next stretch. The visits also give you a peace of mind that all is good at home. Once the kids update me on all that they are doing and what their plans are, we do a rundown on the whole family.

I try not to discuss myself too much and if I do say anything, I usually wait until the end of the visit.

My friend Freddy's two children have children and he was able to see one of them last week at a visit. It's was really great to see him beaming with happiness. Warren's family came up from Louisiana and they had a nice visit. Your people may be from all over the country.

My children are now in three different schools, so it's difficult to make that trip together. They've done a pretty decent job of coordinating to make that happen. I must say that once I became accustomed to not having any visits, I was okay. It's hard to wrap your head around that it's actually okay. It's not the end of the world if you don't have any visits, but it sure is nice when you do.

You put yourself in the camp, your family did not do it for you. Can you imagine how hard this is for them to visit you in a place like this? It's embarrassing and extremely difficult.

While many people think that the camp is like an HBO bad prison movie, it's not. USP maybe more like that bad prison movie, so when your family sees you in a camp, they may be relieved that you are not in too bad of a spot and that you're doing okay.

Over the last several months, John and I have been doing our countdown to our departure date. The date that we can go home. I am a week or so behind him, but too close to worry about the weekly pulls. He works at the warehouse and has a desk. Around the desk, are large orange cards that he made into a countdown calendar. Each Wednesday, not sure why Wednesday, except that it's his exact date, we pull down a number. This week, it was 27, which left 26 weeks until we go home. He has other calendars, as well. He even counted out peanut M&Ms in a jar with the weeks that are left. Each Wednesday, he eats one. He has 26 peanut M&Ms left. Nobody really likes camp and he's definitely one of them. He, along with a few others, has passed time walking, which is pretty easy and truly relaxing.

My visit was really good. Since I have been at the camp, this was their third visit. For some reason, this visit was the best. We laughed, told stories, and were just being "us". I miss them and I think they have missed me.

During this particular visit, Dave and his family were seated at the tables next to us in the visitor's room. He commented to me later that he could see how much we loved each other. He also told me that my persona in the camp was very different from what he observed in the visitor's room. I thought it was nice of him to reflect his observation to me.

While my kids were visiting, I told them that there were some items that needed to be addressed prior to being released. Since my living arrangements had fallen out of place, I needed to have some clothes delivered to where I would be staying. I needed the window on my car fixed and an inspection done. The car also needed a tune up. I didn't want to be driving around in a vehicle that was not inspected. It would not be advisable considering if I were to be pulled over, it would be a violation and putting myself at risk. I can't imagine pulling up to my PO's office with a cracked window and my plates expired.

I recommend that you have prepared for your release before it actually happens. When you're stepping outside of the camp for the first time, no matter the amount of time you've served, your ducks need to be in a row. You really will be blinded by the light and don't want to be stepping out there like someone whose gone cold turkey from a bad habit.

Make sure your driver's license is up to date and accessible to you when you are released, have your clothes and personal items delivered to where ever you are staying, and have access to some cash and transportation. You also need to make sure you have a cell phone lined-up, as well. This will help make your release a smooth transition. You just wasted a lot of time doing absolutely nothing and for some of us, we want a great starting point to build off of. Once that door opens to your freedom, you will want to hit the ground running.

Hopefully, you will have some plans in place, some ideas on the horizon, your family to reconnect with. All of this will take time, energy, and resources. There will no longer a reason to sleep all day or feel sorry for yourself. You're now a free man and it's time to make a real difference in your life. It's up to you to have made the necessary changes, nobody else.

When my wife and kids were getting ready to leave, I told them that I really enjoyed the visit but that there was no need to come back if they were too busy or couldn't coordinate it. I would leave it up to them and that I would love it if they could, but I would have a release date within the next 30 to 60 days. Charlie was my line-up for transportation on out of here. Although, that's my hope. When you're in a place like this, you never know from one day to the next what people on the outside are really committed to do for you, or even how they will act towards you.

When all is said and done, this visit without a doubt, was the best that I had and hoped that it was equally the best that kids had experienced. At the end of the visit, I could feel the connection that I felt was missing, and this time, it was really strong. I shared with them that in the big picture, from my perspective, compared to those that I've met over the past year, 27 weeks was a mere drop in the bucket. You can do that with your eyes closed. Just like a backstroke, you don't put too much thought into it, really. The end of your time in camp will be here before you know it.

It's so important to enjoy each visit that you get. Remember the time commitment that your loved one or friend is making to visit, not to mention the expense. As I mentioned previously, a visitor can really find so many more things to do that really could be more attractive, than driving a distance to sit in a plastic chair in a prison visiting room. Not to mention where they can spend that money besides on coming to see you. Since they are making an effort for you, be appreciative of what time and expense that are providing you.

What a great day! I'm happy at the moment, as you will be too!

Going Home Pizza Party- Camp

There is a little tradition that has been taking place for a while now. You want to give your bunkmate and friend a send-off. It sure isn't a barbeque in your backyard with a bunch of friends, but for what you have available to you, you can do something pretty darn close.

We have many going away parties for our friends. Just remember that every time you have one, you are just one step closer to going home. The goal is for you to have your pizza party! Before too long, you'll know that you want that pizza party. You can pretty much do just about most anything and surely make about anything. Unfortunately, it's not like we are able to order Domino's Pizza. We are able to buy wings from the commissary, though. You can also get cheese, pepperoni, chicken, and sauce from the warehouse. Sometimes we can get these items free, but sometimes we have a small fee. Either way, it makes it convenient for throwing these pizza parties.

There is this guy Billie, or Papa John, as we call him. Billie was arrested while working at Papa Johns. He was still in his uniform when they brought him in; hence why we refer to him as Papa John. We get him involved in the pizza parties and he can whip up the best microwave camp pizza you can find in any of the USP camps. He has a secret ingredient that makes it especially good. Or maybe, our craving for pizza and the occasion makes it over the top.

My bunkmate, Tony, left yesterday. We had a nice size pizza party. Billie made 4 nice pizzas and we invited about 20 people. We use what we have ingredients and_make something different and special. So, we were all set. Everyone brings their own drink and a plate. A plate is typically the top off of a storage container that you can buy from the commissary. Sometimes you just have to be innovative and realize that it's the best that it's going to get.

We gathered together to have a nice send off. They're always so nice. We were out on the patio right off the visitor's room. Every night, someone is using it, whether it is to read, do yoga, just to sit around and relax. Tonight, we were using it for Tony's sendoff pizza party, which was a little different than most nights. The CO was in a bad mood because some campers were talking during the count. You know, kids will be kids and there is not much that you can do about it.

Graham grabbed the microwave, I guess to heat up the pizza. That was the straw that broke the camel's back. The CO came out and told us that nobody was allowed outside tonight and if he caught anyone, they would be written up. What a jerk. We moved the party inside and put the microwave back where it belonged. It was probably for the best since it was cooler inside and there were no bugs. We had our party and it was nice. Afterwards, we did a little clean up and we all went about our business. Tony went around the camp, collecting some addresses, said his goodbyes, and did a little packing. He was leaving at 8:00 a.m. in the morning.

At 7:30 a.m., we walked out front and waited for the CO to give him his release papers. He was going to a halfway house for a few weeks. Hey, good for him, at least he was out of here. His mother was waiting for him outside. Once all of the paperwork was signed, we all walked over to his mother's car. It was a brief but nice farewell. She cried and was so happy it was finally over with for him. It was a nice feeling.

I'm up next, then it will be your turn. One more day down, that's always good news.

Freedom

Bye Bye-Freedom

No matter what you have done, right or wrong, guilty or innocent. If a judge has sentenced you, well you've owned up to the responsibility and you're preparing for the next phase of your life. Depending on your age, it could seem like you've been serving a life sentence. You've hung in there; have kept the hope and you know that you are going home sometime down the road.

You've endured the disgrace that you have handed to your family, friends, and community. I know this was the lowest point in my life, and most likely yours, as well, whether you admit to it or not. Understand that rebuilding your life once you've been released, is just a new chapter. Now is the time to prepare yourself for the changes that are coming your way. Your life will not be the same. Good, bad, or indifferent. You went in leaving a life behind and soon you will be coming out and things will most certainly be different. If this realization hasn't occurred, you may be faced with some troubles in the horizon. Do you have any idea as to what to expect? It could be like a blind man leading the blind.

Your time will come, it will time to go…be prepared to say so long…you'll find yourself looking from the outside soon.

The Final Exit- Freedom

The time has finally arrived! I am going to walking out of the door to a new level of freedom. I was beginning to think that I would ever get out of here. It's only days away and I feel like celebrating life at the camp. Unfortunately, there is no food from the warehouse or the commissary, so there won't be a pizza party. Since I don't have access to the internet and the phone is too expensive, I won't be contacting my friend and family to share my great news.

I didn't work at the halfway house so I hung out at the building in the residence hall all day, which was a real drag. Watching television and taking naps really helps pass the time, but you can only do so much of that. There is not a real library and I did not buy any books when I went to Walmart, so that didn't help occupy my mind.

After listening to the many stories, maybe they're just tall-tales, from other campers, I found some of them very entertaining. I soaked them up. Let me tell you, you will hear some really good stories. I know I enjoyed reveling in many of them.

The days are long but the nights much longer. Last night, it felt like I never slept. I was too excited because I knew that I was finally leaving and I felt great. My mind was going in a million different directions. I kept thinking about all of the things I was going to do when I got back home. I have yards to mow and rent to collect. I am sure there will be renovations that need to take place. None of the properties were ever maintained while I was at camp, this was eating away at me this whole time. I would to have like to have had the rent monies saved up for my return but that's obviously not what happened.

I thought that I had it all organized for the time I was going away. Unfortunately, it took the individual who was supposed to be helping me 90 days to drive the properties into the ground. To top it all off, he stole the rent money. I went through several others that I thought I could trust but it turned into an absolute nightmare. I had Ed, a friend of mine, or so I thought, run the properties for the kids. I found out that he was using my office to have sex with some of the female tenants. He pocketed the rent money and never did any repairs on the properties. When I got home, I discovered that out of the 23 properties, only two were occupied. The rest were boarded up, the taxes hadn't been paid, and all of the utilities were cut off. My office was turned upside down, it was a disaster. The only bank account that I had a balance in when I left, was down to a penny and two days later, he sucked that penny out and closed the account. What was once a trusted friend was not an evil being that took full advantage of me and my situation. It was crushing. Keep in mind that I had my plan in place but didn't have a plan B in order. If you have business to take care of while you are incarcerated, always have a plan B. All you can do if you inherit a similar situation as mine, is take it one day at a time to rebuild. Don't run away!

It doesn't matter where you are, whether you have a little or a lot, or nothing at all, you still have to be excited to be on your way to what I consider "partial freedom". I know I felt like a little kid waiting for Santa Claus, as I could hardly contain myself.

I feel that I have a good plan in place and I know that things will be ok. You know you've had plenty of time to think about your plan, now it's time to execute it.

It's only a matter of the wake-up call now and this path on my journey will be over. The hardest part of the next phase is that I will still be away from my family and friends, and not being in my own bed. I am looking forward to my own bed, pillow, and taking a real shower. It's funny how it's the little things that we take for granted. Being able to sit around in my boxers if I want to and just being able to live my life is something that I know I will never take for granted again.

Out The Door- Freedom

The day has finally come and when my name was finally called, I let out a great big sigh of relief. This was feeling that I realized I had never really experienced before, at least, not to this extent. Being cooped up for 21 months really felt like an eternity, I almost felt like a lifetime had passed me by. I was about to enter the next phase of this nightmare. Believe me, even thought I had to acclimate and got through it, it was still a nightmare. One that will probably haunt me for the rest of my life.

I opted out of the BOP clothes, as I planned to be picked up at the bus station by my friend Charlie. A comedy of errors thwarted that plan. I was not given enough time to get from the camp to the halfway house. Even though the BOP used Google Maps it just seemed to be possible so I decided to take the bus. I wasn't looking for any trouble at this stage of the game.

The bus was to leave Morgantown traveling to Union Station in D.C. with a 4-hour layover, then to Richmond, Roanoke, and then Bristol, where I was to take a taxi to the halfway house in Lebanon. It didn't seem to complicated. Charlie had called the camp to get approval to pick me up at the bus station. Apparently, that's against the rules and if you don't adhere to this rule, you are considered breaking the conditions of your furlough. I don't recommend this, after all, you have worked too hard and have come too far to risk trouble at this point. I'm sure you will agree.

I know I disappointed Mark and a few of the other guys at the camp. You know they always say there is a time and place for everything. Be as patient as you can. I know I am doing what is asked of me and what I need to do. Where ever you end up, you will make promises to people and for different reasons. Whatever it may be, under whatever circumstances, you always want to do what you say that you are going to do. Even though you may never see anyone from camp or prison again, you still have to live with yourself. Take care of your commitments and once you've lived up to them, you will be able to move on.

I said a few goodbyes, put my things in Dave, the town driver's car. It was for real; it was time for me to leave. We drove down the entrance way and made a right turn to freedom. We got onto the interstate and headed towards Morgantown. Dave was in the front with me and Cooper, another camper, was in the back. No, it didn't take two of them to take me but when you're a town driver, you're going to take any opportunity to leave camp, even if it's for an hour or so.

Dave asked me how I felt. I couldn't really express it. I wasn't overwhelmed, nor did an aura overcome me all at once, but I was feeling completely cleansed. I was wearing real clothes in the first time in a long time. I was reveling in seeing activity on the outside of the walls of a prison camp for the first time in a very long time. I am really breathing in what I am considering free air, even though the camp was just a few miles behind me, the air hasn't been essentially free to anyone there. This was the air of freedom. I felt like a new person. Shedding those greens and sweats. No more same smell, the same look, and I was feeling like I could stretch my arms without anyone making a snide remark or two. This was fabulous.

Dave and Cooper really wanted some boneless chicken strips from KFC but Dave could not remember where the restaurant was, which didn't surprise me. We got to the bus station but hadn't eaten and I realized I was hungry too. You know you will be dying to eat something that you haven't had in a very long time. You most likely won't be picky, anything will do. Since my drivers had to go back to the camp, I thought I would treat them to lunch. I could eat later if I needed to. I had all of the time I need and I was feeling good.

Dave found a Chick-fil-A because he really wanted chicken tenders. We pulled in and I went in since I was essentially a free man and I had the cash. It was just like riding a bicycle. I went up to the counted and ordered our lunch which was a family pack of chicken tenders, 24 of them, served on a catering tray. I felt like I was taking them to a special gathering or family buffet.

We noshed on them for a few minutes. They were hot and so tasty. I could feel Dave getting antsy and he wanted to get back. I had not finished my treat but that was ok, I was happy to leave the rest of them with Dave and Cooper, they deserved them. Afterall, I was most likely to have all of the chicken tenders I would want. So, Dave took me to what he thought was the bus ticket area at the bus station. It was nothing more than a parking garage and main station for the bus lines, such as Greyhound or Megabus. Dave really had no idea where he was supposed to go or where he was taking me. He and Cooper left and there I was with my small bag and three extremely heavy boxes that contained all of my writings. I asked several people where the next bus was going to come in at but I never received a definite answer. I looked around, there were no signs for either bus line, just a weather pavilion with no seats. Isn't this just typical, par for the course? I'm not sure, but I will say this, don't just assume that your trip will be without its challenges.

I bought a Diet Coke, which was the one thing I was really craving. I settled in for my 2-hour wait for a bus that I wasn't even sure was going to come in. Even if Charlie where to have come, they moved me from a Greyhound to a Megabus. I found out that the Greyhound station was on the other side of town. The BOP really may try to trip you up, confuse you, and trust me, they've done a good job of that! It was really hot outside but the heat felt good. I was still not sure if Charlie was going to show up at any given moment. I was at this bus station (if that's what you want to call it) looking around and feeling amazed that I was even here. I started to get a little paranoid, thinking that people were scoping me out. I even thought maybe the BOP had put a CO in the parking lot to make sure that I was getting on the bus. I am sitting on this wall in 90* heat waiting for a bus. I am traveling on a Megabus. Nobody else is standing around and I really don't even know if I am where I am supposed to be. I had the three boxes and this bag and was very thirsty. I've become accustomed to being cautious but I left them for a few minutes anyway and found a cheap variety store for a drink. I asked this goofy guy behind the counter if the Megabus was always on time and if I were in the right spot to catch it.

I wanted to make a phone call to Charlie to see if he were somewhere in the area or if he were at home. I hadn't spoken with him in a few days and I knew I needed to call to break the ice. I was afraid to ask anyone to borrow their phone. Payphones no longer existed because everyone has a cell phone in their pocket. I finally see a guy standing there and I ask him if I can borrow his phone for a minute. Wow, I was impressed, these new cell phones are great, but unfortunately for me this guy's phone was in Chinese. By the time I figured it out, he needed to catch his bus, and I didn't get that call in. I paced around for a bit, trying to concoct a plan, but came up empty. I decided to go back into the terminal and found someone who was kind enough to allow me to make my call.

Charlie answered his phone on the second ring. I gave him heads up, shared the details of what was going on. He was in Richmond, just hanging out. Well, geez, isn't that just fine and dandy, as I continue to wait for a Megabus in the sweltering heat, wondering if it were even going to show up. I did not even care, really, I was just happy I was out of the camp where I was beginning to really feel like I was trapped, getting frustrated and annoyed with the system, as well as the people. The timing of my release was just perfect. I hung up the phone with Charlie and went back to waiting. The time was slowly dragging on but I was thinking about the bus connections, what I was going to eat first, and asking myself why I didn't grab a few of those chicken tenders!?

The bus pulled in a few minutes early at 5:15. It was obvious that it was a Megabus because the logo was all over it. People got off of it and out of nowhere people were everywhere, going in multiple directions. My best guess was that an additional 10 people boarded the bus. The driver was kind enough to help me with my heavy boxes and put them in the storage area. I showed him my itinerary and was surprised that there was no ticket to punch. Guess what, there were no COs in the parking lot either. Someone could have easily picked me up and nobody would ever have known it. It was smooth sailing right on out of there. I guess as long as you are able to get to where you are supposed to be and on time, that's really all that matters.

I boarded the bus and settled into a lounge seat in the back, by myself. I was so happy to be free, alone, and comfortable. I welcomed the comfortable seat and being alone. Of course, having a friend or family member picking me up would have been an awesome feeling, this was equally as wonderful. The bus finally took off and made its way through Morgantown and onto the interstate. It had been a while since I have seen the sights, all of the retail stores that pepper the edge of the highway, there were cars, trucks, and motorcycles, all containing people who were out and about. Oh, how we take all of this for granted. I am so grateful to be on my way to freedom. I sat in my comfortable seat and reflected on the past two years of my life, as well as what I have planned for the future. The future is going to be great! I know that nothing will stop me, the past 10 years were absolutely horrible and all of those people who let me down really made me see who I can really trust. So many people took advantage of me for all of those months. It's well forgotten for now and maybe they will be held accountable at some point in their lives.

We were about 2 hours into the drive to Union Station, D.C. when we pulled off for a break. We were at a nice Pilot Travel Center where there was an Arby's. I wandered up and down the aisles and much to my surprise, I really didn't see anything that I really wanted to buy. I did end up buying a ¼ lb. hotdog with no bun. I haven't had a really good hotdog in forever, it smelled good but was only subpar. The break came to a close and we all got back on the bus to complete the journey to D.C. I once again settled in for some more peace and quiet. No more counts, no more yelling, no more banging or loud noises, and no more metal bunk beds. No more craziness…it was all behind me now. I couldn't help but to let out another great big sigh, sat back and closed my eyes with a big smile on my face.

We finally arrived at Union Station at 10 p.m. and I had a 4-hour layover. The lady at the counter was nice enough to let me leave my things so I didn't have to lug them around. I walked around this huge terminal looking for something to eat. I had asked Marcus from camp once about the "who's, what's, and where's" at this station, but apparently, he didn't have a clue because the paces he told me about did not even exist. My only options were McDonalds and an Au Pan Bakery. I went for the Au Pan and had very nice chicken sandwich with a diet iced tea. I ate and relaxed a little bit, then walked around and did some window shopping. This place was filled with some really nice stores, some of them expensive, so it was a nice treat, considering I haven't been in a retail store in two years. I will say to have to kill 4 hours was a little tough so I decided to venture out of the station and walked around some. I was able to get a great view of the White House and took a moment to reflect on our justice system and how unjust it is. It's difficult not to feel bitter about it, but I can only hope that at some point in time they will revamp the systems and put the crimes committed into perspective when they are handing out sentences.

I could not help but to think of those who I had met that had huge sentences for conspiracy, then there are those who were given lengthy sentences for something they did wrong that may be considered relatively small in the grand scope of things. Then there are murderers who don't ever get caught. We can only hope that with time the problems will be resolved.

All of those strongarmed prosecutors with their tactics threaten people into taking pleas. This is intimidating. Then they move onto your loved ones, threatening them to pressure to make a deal. It goes on and on. I spent some time thinking about the many people, friends that I left behind that have not much time left. I think about their wellbeing and peace of mind.

The Greyhound arrived at the terminal on time at 2 a.m. It was a very impressive, brand-new bus. It was almost full, with only four vacant seats. I was third in line and could not risk being bumped. That would make me late for the next bus in Richmond. That would interfere with my scheduled arrival to be at the halfway house, SECOR, in Lebanon, Virginia. Even if you are 15 minutes late, you are considered an escapee. All I know is that it was making me anxious because I did not want anything to interfere with me going home. Remember, you're in new, uncharted territory. You have no idea what you are in for. Nobody will tell you anything and you are they even know anything to begin with. Either way, don't expect not to get anxious. What you need to remember is that you are completing this journey. You now know that you are close to the door and the halfway house, or whatever you are going to experience will be the last step to your freedom.

My care manager at Hazelton did not prepare me for anything. What was odd is that there is a huge emphasis on re-entry into society and your world. I have found that there are only a few people out there that will tell you the truth of what to expect. If you feel betrayed and lied to right from the get go, I don't blame you one bit. I was told I would be at the halfway house for a few days, then I would go home with the possibility of electronic monitoring. The PO approved the house I was going to stay at. I had a job and I really thought all of my basis covered.

I completed my trip and arrived at SECOR, where I was 15-minute ahead of schedule. Before I get into my discussion about that, I must share a moment of a special cab ride from the Bristol bus station to SECOR in Lebanon, Virginia, which was a 45-minute ride. This was not your typical yellow taxi cab, but a car with a cardboard sign duct taped to the roof of it. Two guys were in the front. One who was missing most of his teeth and barely spoke a word of English and the other reeked of alcohol. Oh boy, are you kidding me? I couldn't help but to chuckle. At this point, I didn't even care, I just wanted to keep going. The trip started out slowly and I noticed that the gas gauge was on empty, so I piped up and suggested that they get gas before we went too much further. The driver agreed and then asked me for the $85 cab fare in advance. I couldn't help but to wonder where these two even came from and prayed that I got to SECOR in one piece and on time. The back window was broken and the cold wind was blowing into the backseat. Even though it was the dead of summer, that particular early morning, it was cold enough to chill a polar bear. Heh, they could care less and really why would they?

The halfway house, SECOR, has got to be better than those I have heard horror stories about from many of the inmates I met in camp. Hope Village in DC is supposed to be pretty bad, so is the one in Baltimore. I was holding my breath, but realistically, at this point, I think anything would be better than camp or a prison, and besides, I am supposed to only be here a few days and am designated for home confinement with an ankle monitor. I was onboarded and had my orientation and was told by the care manager, Sherry, that the BOP, and my case manager at Hazelton had it all wrong. What? Wrong after 21 months and the countless team meetings, how is that they had it all wrong? Then I realized that this was no surprise, after all that I have been through, as the others have been through the same, it should almost be expected. I had thought the BOP was in charge. It seems like there are a lot of people, but not one particular person, is in charge.

At one point, I was beginning to feel like a hamster on a wheel, just going around and around, you're not looking for exercise, just a way out. There is a door on the cage, but the question is, who will open it for you. SECOR has been around for a long time, so have the people who run it. They all seem to be nice, local country people, who have multiple roles and responsibilities. They are counselors, intake specialists, drivers, care managers, pill dispensers, secretaries, among others. There are three individuals that work here that I have resonated with. They seem to be able to get things done. Bobby, Rhonda, and Sherry seem to be dependable. I'm not sure about the rest, unless I consider Myrtle, who has a horrific, nasty attitude. Maybe it just goes with the territory, I guess. While it shouldn't be, after all, why be nasty when it takes less energy to be nice. I'm just attempting to get to the next step.

After my orientation, I get settled into my bunk, which is a spring type bed, one that you would find in earlier military days, or what you would find at an old roadside motel. Nothing too terribly special, but much better than the metal bunk at the camp. I wish I had brought my pillow from camp, this one here is like laying your head on shredded cardboard wrapped up in a vinyl cover. I welcome the change, especially since there are no standup counts. It took me a minute to disenfranchise myself from the 10 a.m., 4 p.m., and 9 p.m. counts. I caught myself looking at the time over and over again and realized that it was close to count time. I just went about my business and didn't think about it again. What a nice change!

There are three levels of bed time and privileges at SECOR. Level 1 requires you to be in your room by 9 p.m., Level 2 requires you to be in your room by 10 p.m., and with Level 3, you are required to be in your room by midnight, hey that's not so bad, is it? I was given a Level 2 bedtime, that worked for me. I typically turn in about that time because I am worn out from watching ridiculous sitcoms and the news. None of this works for me but what other choice do I have. I don't care to get caught up in the bad news, but unfortunately, that is all these places have is more bad news, and plenty more broken promises. All I can do is sit there and listen, think about what I should say, and carefully state my case. If you provide a solution without being disrespectful, it may be your only chance. Remember it is them against you. You are only one of the many that they have seen with a similar story. There will be many more coming in after you leave, so just remember your story will hold little to no value.

The SECOR housing unit looks like an old office building that was converted to accommodate both male and female recipients. About 50% are federal inmates that should better assessed and some need to be there because they have lost some their social and living skills. They are way too many that should just be sent home. There is so much overkill. If you don't get the deal now, you many never get it. There are way too many trouble makers that will never get it right. They will be detained for even more trouble when they get out. The converted office building has private rooms, with 2 men per room, which is nice. There are old bathrooms, an inadequate laundry room, a mail room and T.V. room with 2 vending machines and a lot of noise. Recreation is basically walking around the building. It's not impressive to say the least, but remember this is a short-term stay. There was an addition that was built onto the front of the building and I am almost certain that the person who constructed it is very proud of what they created. With some more thought, they could have really made it nice, but that ship has sailed, and they were definitely not on it. A nicer plan would have been to put a second floor above the office to use for facilitating more growth and better accommodations for those who are there.

After about five minutes with anyone in the place, I realized you will get about all of the information that you can tolerate. I listen to some of the stuff people will talk about and while it may be entertaining or intriguing, most of it goes in one ear and out of the other. Some of it is worthless to you and it won't even matter. Think about it this way, you're not there to make life-long friends, you're just existing, and like in camp, it's best to stay below the radar. Do what you have to do to get through it.

The job search is sort of a joke. There are way too many residents than there are openings in this area. The area is inundated with applicants, and some businesses are willing to hire a few of us, while others do not even want to talk to you. There may be 10 people applying for one job at the Bonanza, which is crazy. I think that is a little disorganized and not very effective for the purpose, but as you know, my opinion does not hold any merit, so I've learned to keep it to myself.

The days come and go. The surroundings that were all so new start to pull you down to a level of despair. As far as a re-entry program is concerned, it does seem to be way off base. There are all of these case workers walking around, some of them really care, while others do not. There is never the same answer given by two people for the same question, everyone has their own opinion about what they think the answer should be, right or wrong. I just gave someone .75 cents to buy a soda, go figure. That seems somewhat odd. They are telling me not to lend anyone anything, especially money. You may get it back but I am resolved to knowing that I may not. Take it from me, you may just not want to put yourself out there like that. This place doesn't have any refrigerators for snacks. There is no ice, only the vending machines that get crushed every day. Some guys just sit around all day, snacking.

I am fighting total boredom, daily. It's totally nuts because I feel like at least at the camp, there was more to be involved with. I really thought that the halfway house would have been totally different. If possible, line up a job before you get to the halfway house. I've found that would have been the way to go. If your PO did a home inspection, you would want to be sure that it is sent out to all of the right people and the is just not sitting on it. That the worst. Try to be as professional as possible. If you can, be as nice as possible so that he will send out his report promptly. I'm telling you this because it's almost as if you are doing his job for him, but he's getting paid, not you. For some reason, mine was done for the job, as well as the home inspection but nobody received it at SECOR. Of course, it's just like anything else in this world, they find only the things that are convenient for them to find, and then it stops there.

I will admit, I was becoming frustrated being at the halfway house. There many people who really need to be here, I am not one of them. There are those who really need assistance in finding a job, securing housing, maybe receive basic skill training, or even basic life experience before getting back into society. I did not need any of this because I was classified for in home confinement. Even though I was told by my case worker at Hazelton, along with his boss that I would only be here for a few short days, I have found out that this is far from reality. Another reason that I cannot stress enough that you really cannot believe anything you've been told. Don't trust what you are being told. They are either really lousy at their jobs or they don't have any moral compass and will lie to you with a straight face. Don't listen to the ex-cons that are at the halfway house with you, because they're full of beans. Not everyone's case looks the same, so what may be available to Joe, may not be available to you. I must say I feel like I was set up for yet another disappointment. I only have myself to blame. So, I'm here to tell you, don't take your plans to the next level until you know what things really look like for you. The reality is that the halfway houses are a part of the system and there is really no care about your future or anyone else's. Just because the BOP clarifies that you have been a model camper that you are good to go because there will be many obstacles that will stand in your way. Don't be surprised if you find yourself frustrated with the halfway house agenda.

Much of the problem is money. The halfway house typically gets paid by the government for your time there. They get paid 25% of your gross wages if you are working. There are some that will release you if you have a job at home and are able to double and even triple dip into their income by renting your bed out again. I would suspect that there is a deeper deception that exists. I'm pretty certain the government prosecutes the few that they want and really allows most of the people to rip them off. The mad rant is that they get away with it. It's a problem that's been present in the system for years.

It will not take you log to fit in and figure the halfway house out. You are experienced in now with fitting in and becoming part of a new culture. I must say that part was not bad for me. Many of the guys for the most part, were pretty decent. There were only two of them that were real jerks, there is always someone who has to act stupid. It's just the same games people play, just in a different environment. There are different faces attached to many of the same names that other people you have met share. What's pretty cool is that this place is your ticket to freedom. Once you are done with the halfway house time, you are no longer an inmate. You have paid your price to society. The people at SECOR are friendly, they do the best they can to help. They answer the questions to the best of their ability. What is bad is that they are not getting the federal people out because they need the money. Be prepared, there are really silly rules that you will have to follow. Don't take in a cell phone and stay away from alcohol. Someone just got in trouble for having a chair in the hallway. There are cameras everywhere and there is a crazy loudspeaker. You may find yourself really confined to your room or a crowded day room. I find it to be a little claustrophobic. In less than a month, I felt like climbing the walls, but what I focused on was that the nightmare was just about over.

The Big Burger Experience-SECOR

I feel that it's necessary to share with you more about SECOR, because you may end up here.

This halfway house may be unique from all of the other halfway houses. What I would bet on is that all the halfway houses are all unique and they're really all the same. SECOR is not a halfway house but a detention center. It's a step down from a regular prison. They are strict and have many stupid rules, half of them are unspoken rules. It's just hearsay, really. Some of them are really not logical, at all.

I found out after the fact, that if you apply for a job at a supermarket and have finished the process but decide to buy laundry soap while you are there, you are breaking a rule. When you go somewhere, whether it is to work, to dinner, or to make a purchase, according to the rules at SECOR, you cannot go anywhere else. You really have little freedom. None of this is in writing. It's all passed down to you, word of mouth, and if you're smart enough to ask, you may get an understanding of how things work before you make a mistake. The case workers at SECOR are another story. I am just not sure that they are even college educated because nobody displays them in their offices. Even though they did their best, I'm not sure some of them even have the experience to fill the job requirements. Most of them are unprofessional and show no consideration for others. Some of them would eat their fast food while they were supposed to be meeting with you. While this may seem trivial, it was conducive to other bad habits and behaviors that were visible to all of us. It's been an eye-opening experience, that's for sure.

I only have six ore days left at SECOR, so I decided I would at least attempt another job search. I spent some time doing some research, which is part of the requirements. Keep in mind, I'm just going through the motions because I have a job when I am finally able to go home. I am on a home confinement status. The only reason to land a job is to have an excuse to get something to do. The only options are Wendy's, Pioneer, Food City, and Bonanza. I had a pass to check on my application for employment at Food City. I had this buddy in SECOR who I walked with. We decided to eat lunch somewhere together. He had not eaten at the Pioneer, and I had been there two days prior. I think they have awesome hamburgers that they serve with crinkle fries. So, we decided to go to the Pioneer, figuring this would be the last meal together. We set the lunch date up for the Thursday before I was to leave.

Five days before I was supposed to leave, the bus rolls up at its usual 1:30 p.m., we both check out and left for our lunch date. The oversized van that was outfitted as a bus, went all over town and it took about a half hour until we finally pulled up to Food City. I politely asked the substitute driver if he would wait for me and he said he would. I ran inside, found someone in customer service to sign my job placement sheet. I quickly walked outside, only to find that the bus had left. I was feeling a little queasy so I went to the restroom. I ended up at the fresh hot deli bar to check out what was for lunch. I had eaten there the week before and had some tempura Talapia and some chicken fingers. It was a very nice meal and I was full and happy, to say the least.

I was walking though the store only to see Keith running around frantically looking for me. He was my partner in crime and had the bus circling the parking lot, waiting for me. He wasn't going to leave me hanging and miss our lunch date at the Pioneer. We drove the rest of the route and descended onto the Pioneer, where we both got out. I asked the bus driver if would like a milkshake, and he said no. Ok, suit yourself, I thought to myself. Keith and I went to the counter and ordered our burgers and crispy fries, along with a drink. While it was being prepared, Keith put in his application and had his job research paper signed. We were good to go. Keith wanted some chew, so we needed to go to the convenience store next door to the Pioneer, so we walked over and he bought his tobacco. He was happy. You know it seemed as harmless as nothing, right? What was the harm? There were no written rules that said we could not go, right?

We went back over the Pioneer and our order was up. It smelled great. We went over to the concrete tables and sat down on a concrete bench. We divided up the food and dug in. We were having a big time eating and enjoying our lunch. At that moment, I turned to the left and saw a black car sitting there. I looked a little harder and saw that the driver was Rita, who was the director at SECOR. She asks what we are doing and I respond that we are having lunch, a burger and fries. I almost slipped and offered her some, but I didn't. I think she was in shock that I answered her honestly and nonchalantly. Why wouldn't I, we didn't have anything to hide. Rita was downright nasty and asks me why I was at the Pioneer and not at Food City, where I signed out for. I told her I got sick and the computers at Food City were tied up. I was headed back to SECOR but decided to help Keith out by introducing him to the manager at the Pioneer. Rita was stunned and asks me if I know the manager, and I explained that I met him last week when I put in an application last week. Really, Rita? Why not, honestly, the element of surprise cannot hurt, and that's what we did. Keith pipes up and tells Rita that we were hungry and there was nothing in the rule book that said we could not eat. She was visibly irritated. Keith was as cool as a cat. I was nervous and could not eat. She told us not to go anywhere, that she was calling SECOR to have us picked up. Really? Keith kept eating and I ended up throwing mine in the trash.

My mind immediately went to the worse of the worse. May even losing my eligibility for home confinement. I had crossed the line, pushed the envelope too far, no I am not kidding. Do you see how they trip you up? This is what they do at SECOR. While Keith kept on enjoying his food, I wasn't feeling very good at all. I started to speak negatively to myself, reminding myself of my own stupidity. I took a chance, got caught and now I did not know what the price would be.

Here came nasty Myrtle to take us back to SECOR. As always, she was oblivious to what was going on. We arrived safe and sound at SECOR, only to relay the story to the other residents, many of them thought it was funny. We were now nicknamed the Burger Boys, the Burger Bandits, and the Pioneer Boys. James gave me hell, which I deserved. He had warned me and I didn't listen. Go figure, right? It's just what I do. We waited and waited; it took about an hour before I heard my name being called over the loud speaker. Oh boy, here I go. I was unpleasantly greeted by the day staff only to be told that Rita was expecting me in her office. There she was, all poker faced, sitting there with Sherry who had a disappointed look on her face. I took a deep breath, I was ready to face the music, lay it on me. There was the E.M. sheet on her desk. I was waiting for the hammer to drop.

She asked a few stupid questions that I answered and managed to peel off an apology. Well to my surprise, I got my exit date. 6 more days and I was leaving this den of death and despair. Another sense of relief flooded over me. It was real, the nightmare that I had been living was soon coming to a close. I am going to go home and live my life. I was amazed. I knew I had done something that could have bought me more time but hey I put that behind me, I am going home.

It didn't matter that I had a lot on my plate that was not being dealt with. Even with an ankle monitor, it has to be better than this. I am hoping that there will be less restrictions and more freedom to obtain, I have business to take care of.

I wrote letters to Roland, Dallas, and Charlie. I am hoping Dallas will be at SECOR at 8 a.m. to take me home. I have to be at the PO's office at 11 a.m. This shouldn't be a problem. From there, I will go to Walmart for a phone, that's easy enough, then a treat for Dallas. Going to a hibachi bar is one of our favorite past times. I have not had Chinese for some time and this will be a thrill.

The last couple of days have been tough, only because the days are very long. I can't seem to sleep any of my time away, as much as I wanted to, it just wasn't happening. I bought a CD player so I have enjoyed a few movies, that's helped pass some of my time. Dinner is always at 5 p.m. and then a one hour walk. I am not eating much because I am too excited about leaving. There are a few phones around and have not been able to call Dallas. I did ask Charlie to call him on Friday when he left and he said he would, which was assuring.

I need to get to one of those phones so I can confirm that he is coming. I am sure that he will and he's never late nor does he ever hand out excuses, he just does it. He's a fabulous friend to have.

The nights are getting tougher and tougher. I am wide awake for hours upon hours, just thinking about all that I have to do and want to do. No worries, it will all come together with no hiccups. I am going to the Salvation Army to find Ronell who was at SECOR with me and work with him. I also have Zane, so I will be back in the saddle in no time. Two days to go, come on baby, let's go!

The day finally arrived. Dallas was there on time. I checked out of SECOR with elation and gratitude and started my new life's adventure…more to come.

Just so you know, it won't be an easy transition. You will have to go into recovery mode, become rehabilitated so that you will be able to successfully re-enter society. You will also have to deal with probation or parole, depending on your offense. Here's my guidance and encouragement as you continue your path to being successful in your re-entry process.

Rehab- Recovery

Rehab is something that comes with the territory of going home. You can do this. I didn't have much help…people looked down on me. I felt like people were thinking "he's the guilty one". You may find that you will have to take this journey by yourself.

It doesn't matter how long you have been in custody. Whether you are a stepdown camper, a self-surrender, or a first timer, the problems everyone will face are all similar. The government, through its system, will want to institutionalize you. They want to strip you of your assets and everything else that they can get their hands on. Things that you hold dear to your heart. There is no conscious nor humility in any way or fashion. If you can come out unscathed, you are for the better. If you have become institutionalized, it may be a little more difficult. Who wants to go home and be counted three times a day. It's not easy to get these seemingly little things out of your headspace. Don't get caught by your family standing by your bed at 4 p.m. for count. They may think you're nuts. I know I would.

Maintain some level of normalcy if you can and it will make your return home easier. As I mentioned before, you will always dream while you are camping at the USP. You will find yourself thinking about what you could have done, what you should have done differently. Of course, I am not suggesting that there is a better way of committing a crime, but being able to make better decisions so you would not find your way into the USP.

Your life will not be the same when you get out. I hope that you have not missed out on too much. You will have to find a way to reindoctrinate yourself with your family, the workforce, technology, transportation, your home and relationships. Your short-term and long-term finances, your mental health and even your physical health will need to be adjusted once you've been released. Your mindset, the way you see things will need to be adjusted in a positive light. Nobody can do this but you. Your attitude must be right.

You will find that there will be so many issues you will have to do with upon your release. Things that you may not have even thought of will just pop up. You may be someone who has a knack for survival and that's awesome if you are. Think beyond that, you want to do more than just survive, you want to recover and be successful, legally. It will take hard work and commitment to be able to be successful with your finances, professional life and family growth.

Any of the camps that you would be sent to are not going to a good job in preparing you for your release. Perhaps it's the lack of financial resources that limit them from doing so. Then again, is it up to them? How is it possible to get the criminal, the liar, the thief, or even worse eliminated from someone's behavior? That's a tough question to ponder. The many that have gotten caught, those who were in the wrong place at the wrong time may have it much easier. The camps may have a few programs available. None of the that I've looked into seem to focus on respect, moral or value issues. It's up to you to find the resources to help repair those issues.

Nobody owes you anything. If you want to be respected, you are going to have to go out there and do it yourself. Respect is earned. Walk the straight line rather than demand it and you will be just fine. Don't wait on anyone else to get anything started. You need to take the initiative and make things happen for yourself.

Mark was in a USP reformatory for an armed robbery charge. He was a first timer and trust me, he had learned his lesson. He knew that when he was released, he would never take a walk into another USP prison again. His experience was something that shook him to the core. Once he was released, he was sent to a halfway house in Cleveland, Ohio. He spent 30 days there and during that time, he saw a therapist who helped him examine his anger issues. He had gone through bootcamp in the US Army but received a dishonorable discharge. He had no respect for authority and that's what led him into an act of crime. Recognizing this was a hard pill to swallow but he knew that it was up to him to develop a new mindset. Once his 30 days were completed, he went home to live with his mother and stepfather, who were very supportive. He was able to find a job in a kitchen at a local greasy spoon. His girlfriend stuck by him during his time at the reformatory. His family was supportive. Everyone gave him what he needed to get back on track. Eventually, he moved to a bigger city and found a better job, which allowed him to get his own place and a new vehicle. He eventually moved back to his home town, landed a great job, and bought a home. His experience in the USP was one that he never wants to recreate and he set himself up for successful rehabilitation.

Your rehabilitation is up to you and you alone. There are resources available to assist you when you are on this new journey.

Re-entry Assistance Resources:
- https://lionheart.org/lionheart-programs/houses-of-healing/reentry-programs
- https://www.ssa.gov/pubs/EN-05-10504.pdf
- https://prisonerresource.com/prison-consulting-services/prisoner-reentry-programs/
- https://www.bop.gov/resources/pdfs/reentry_handbook_20170215.pdf
- https://www.voa.org/correctional-re-entry-services
- https://www.justice.gov/archives/reentry/roadmap-reentry

Overcoming Obstacles-Rehabilitation

No matter how in tune we have become with our own productive and ever-growing mindset, we are going to encounter obstacles on our path. Sometimes we may feel like the world is against us, that our goals have been overturned, and there is no way out. The majority of this mindset comes from our "self-talk" and limiting beliefs. Unless it is deemed by a court of law to be the final act, there is really nothing that you cannot overcome.

In this chapter, I am going to explain some of the main reasons why we get so tied in a knot when challenges arise. I have had many, especially when I was sent to prison. I've been absolutely flat broke, not just financially but mentally and emotionally. Yet, here I am once again, successful and at a point in my life that I am able to offer valuable advice and feedback due to my life experiences. The value that comes from that is much bigger than money, alone.

Many of our obstacles become thieves when you don't learn how to deal with them as they roll in. If you allow them to steal your emotions, your clarity, and focus, they take away the ability to examine the bigger picture. They will emotionally and mentally exhaust you and override the most important of initiatives. When you get a chance to reflect on them, once they have occurred and passed, you realize the hindsight. This a beautiful thing. If you can accept advice, feedback, and constructive criticism from another who has had similar experiences, then you will become even the wiser.

Listen to your gut. Humans are lucky. We have a built-in guidance system that is deep within. I refer to it as a gut feeling. Others may consider this intuition or even your conscious. It's not a myth nor is it a magical superpower. It's a primal instinct that ties our brains into a primal state of "fight or flight". Unmanaged, this can manifest into uncontrollable thoughts and potentially create a path for making poor decisions, and this can result in damaging actions. Not know what direction to take or who to turn to can be challenging. Sometimes it helps to put things down on paper. Creating a list of obstacles and examining them to determine how to overcome them. Don't just accept them and sweep them under the rug because they may resurface. Go with your gut, most likely it's right.

When you are re-entering society after being incarcerated, you will find many obstacles that are created. Having a good support system, whether it be family, a counselor, mentor, or even a good friend, will benefit you. If you are lacking family and friends, find a resource that provides counselors, or a volunteer to assist you with creating a path to overcome your challenges. Whether it be finding a lucrative form of work or reliable transportation. Some ex-convicts have issues with addiction or alcoholism, others suffer from challenges due to emotional or mental health issues. These can create big obstacles for successful re-entry into society.

Mark was able to get back on his feet after successfully completing his orientation program at the halfway house, he knew that he needed to change his habits to better himself. That also meant eliminating some of his social circle because some of those individuals were an introduction to potential problems in his life. He worked hard to eliminate challenges and was able to achieve his goals.

Eliminate your limiting beliefs, when you're working out and training your body to be healthy, don't forget to train your mind. Pray daily, meditate, and be grateful, especially because you are no longer on the inside looking out. Focus on what you envision. Don't be afraid to ask for help. Don't allow your ego or your pride stand in your way. You can do this!

Probation

Make no mistake about your hurdle once you've been released from a camp or prison. You've made it through the next phase, most likely, you've completed your time at a halfway house. Over the years, I have seen many good people screw up on their probation and end up right back where they came from. It's absolutely crazy and unimaginable, or at least for me it is. There are so many people that are repeat offenders, I almost feel like people are being set up by the system to fail. They know that you may screw up and they can justify the longer sentence. Nobody I know wants to go back, or at least that's what we like to believe.

Probation terms will vary. Some may be short and others will be faced with years of probation. Dave spent a year in camp and received 5 years of probation. One of the conditions of his probation was that he could not drink. I did not know that he had a problem with alcohol, maybe he was. When you have a condition such as not drinking, there is usually weekly and random testing that will take place. That's a real pain because if you are working, you will have to make time to go test. It's a bigger problem when you don't have transportation. You could have transportation and no job, which could be less stressful. Either way, having to test weekly or being called in for a random test can get old pretty quickly.

Whatever you do, do not mess with your probation officer (PO). You will have so much time to report to him upon your release. Do it, be on time, if not early. Don't expect him or her to become your friend or mentor. From their perspective, your just another number with a different face, but a similar story the person they saw right before you. They have a job to do, there are rules to follow and you're expected to follow the rules. You're not above the rules. The best advice I can give you is to be honest, forth right, develop an open line of communication, and do what is expected of you.

If you are enjoying your freedom then you are by far a winner. Continue on that path by doing what you need to do to avoid violating your probation conditions. You do not want your probation revoked under any circumstances. This is not an easy process and it can wear you out. I think that the intent is to wear you down but seriously they want you to conform to the system. They really don't want you back in their prisons. Stay clean, stay away from alcohol and drugs so that you can have a clear mind. Don't allow yourself to self-destruct and land back in prison or a camp. This will happen if you are not careful of the company you keep or if you are in the wrong place at the wrong time and for the wrong reasons.

What happens when you violate your probation can send you back to prison or camp where you will be forced to complete your sentence. If you have any suspended time in your sentence then you will lose that as well. I am sure you don't want this to happen. I've heard of ex-convicts who have had their probation revoked, and are not only faced with completing their original sentences, but who have had additional sentences added due to the violation of their probation. Who wants that? Not me and hopefully not you.

I've read that many nonviolent offenders can get probation with suspended sentences. Under the Obama administration, there has been a surge of white-collar convictions and people being sent to prison or camps. There is a clear message that is being conveyed. There are campers that were told they will probably get probation and end up with a 10-year sentence. Drew, from Pittsburg, got screwed over. What was wrong with that deal and how was it possible that your lawyer didn't have a clue? That's what nobody could figure out. Was it possible that your attorney knew exactly what he was doing and made a deal with the prosecutor at your expense? Were they saving their trump card for their next case? You bet they did. Attorneys, prosecutors, and judges should spend a month behind bars, or spend some time in the hole to get a feeling for they're doing. After all, aren't they essentially committing crimes along the way? Don't get me wrong, there are plenty of criminals that need to be in camps or prisons, and spend time in the hole. Of course, these places are not filled with angels, if anything the opposite. There are just way too many people who have become victims of an unbalanced and unfair system.

If you are lucky enough to have been given house arrest, this isn't a bad deal. At least you are able to work during the day. You usually have time restrictions that are enforced. You will know when you can leave and when you are expected to be at home. Generally, you are prohibited from leaving your home on the weekends. You must have a hardwired landline telephone at the house so that your PO will be able to communicate with you to verify that you are indeed home. They may also require you to wear an electronic monitor, which is usually an ankle bracelet. This is very effect for tracking your whereabouts. For heaven's sake, do not get the idea that you can cut that off, this will land you back on the inside.

Your path has only just begun. Once again, you've made it thus far, and you will continue to be successful in becoming the model citizen they expect you to be. I am working towards my success and am sure that you will too. I think we both know that being locked up isn't beneficial to anyone. I wish you all of the best for your future endeavors.

Standing Tall- 10 Steps- Success

Life may not go the way you have laid it out in your head. Your blueprint may be a little different than what is actually happening today. A few may be fortunate to ride the road to success with only a few obstacles or speed bumps that may pop up along the way. You can't run away for the inevitable reality that life is adventure and it will have its ups and downs. It's how we react, what we do with what we are handed, with the understanding that it won't be easy. There will be challenges that you will overcome and excel at.

Survival through life is critical. Don't look for the crutches that can provide you with false hope. Remember that whatever move you make, you want to be sure that there is a solid foundation under your feet. You want to make sure that it's one that you can build on every single day that you are blessed with. Find that ladder and start climbing it at your own pace. It's only going to be as hard as you allow it to be.

When you are faced with any type of crisis, there will be several, consider these tips to ensure your success in overcoming any crisis that rears its ugly head.

Stay calm. Don't lose control. You may be faced with a situation that will overwhelm you, but don't allow it to overcome you. It doesn't do you any good to it allow you to take over your life. Don't allow yourself to become your worst enemy. It happens, you know.

First and foremost, know your limitations. You may have climbed the ladder to the top wrung and can't go any further. Yet, understand that not everyone can get to the top. Consider that everyone has their own "top of the ladder". We're not all on the same road to success, it will look different to all of us. Know that when you get off the ladder, as high as you can go is truly a success. It doesn't happen by beating yourself up or comparing yourself to others. We all can't be the President, remember that someone has to be the Vice President.

Seek outside advice. I have had no problems reaching out to others to make sure that I am on the right track. You may feel uncertain about your path or even yourself, or feel uneasy about what you are dealing with. Once you are able to identify your challenges, write down the 10 steps that you need to take in order to overcome these challenges. Examine these 10 steps and list the pros and cons of each of these items. This gives you a chance to really think about them and modify them to make them work for you. Always talk with someone that you know you can trust. Always having a different perspective broadens your own thoughts and give you an opportunity to create additional solutions. Accepting others input will push you to move forward to a greater level of success. Remember that you must stay as you can during this period of your life. You're having to rebuild a sense of self confidence. It's time to become secure with your steps, your actions and trust yourself again. It's ok if things don't work out the way you thought they would. You will learn from this and be able to create another direction when the outcomes don't show up the way you expect them to.

Stay focused on your goals. The longer you stay focused and plow forward, the easier it will become. There will be many temptations on your path, it's your decision, will you fall from your grace and into the hands of those temptations, or will you remain strong and just say no. The ability to choose is freewill. Freewill is your birthright. Make the right choices, man, your future depends on it.

Do you have a great support system? It's always to your advantage to have some sort type of support system. No misery doesn't deserve company, but having the advantage of being able to solve problems, provide answers and solutions, and climbing the ladder to your success, can happen when you have the support you need. My friend Dallas and I have developed a strong bond over the years and have always worked together to brainstorm and throw ideas back and forth to one another. He's been the ideal friend and has offered me support, even before I landed in the camp. Find someone that you can trust and depend on for support.

When I was married to Margaret, I really tried to share my struggles and challenges with her. For some reason, I had a picture in my mind that this was a part of being married, heh. Instead of offering me support, I found that she didn't even understand half of my frustrations or struggles. Over time, I became increasingly frustrated with her and learned that I couldn't even trust her. As we started to grow a part, she became close to my mother. It led to me becoming a hard man out. The confidential conversations we had came full-circle and bit me in the butt because my mother had made privy to them. I just learned that I could not even confide in my wife, who was supposed to be my confidant and best friend.

Have the courage to disconnect from those who only bring toxicity to your life. Believe in yourself and free yourself from anyone that creates an opportunity for you to start second guessing in your own mind. Don't allow other peoples thoughts about you to define who you really are. Accept what you've lost, who you've lost and understand that the purpose of losing them is a benefit, a gift, or even a lesson.

When you are able to face yourself in the mirror, accept who you are and what your shortcomings are, you will be amazed how things will change for you. Once you accept the outcomes of the decisions you've made, you will see that you can only move forward from that point on. Accept the consequences of your actions, take the pain in stride, and learn from it. Grow from it, become better than you once were. Your success is your own. Own it and be proud of it.

A Special Thank You...

Thank you to my children, Roland, Lauren and Patrick, who were hurt the most (as all families hurt during these time). They were able to endure this travesty of life, they seem to have this scar, but it is important to know that taking responsibility is important and life then begins again, not to label folks when they come home but remember it takes a strong person to pick up the pieces of life and move on to greater success.

Thank you to Angie Kendrick, my ghostwriter and editor, for being able to capture the essence of my words and create this book on my behalf.

We encourage everyone who has read this book to contact their local politicians to seek sentencing reform, to create better policies, and anything that is better than what we have in place to bring folks back into society the way it is today. When folks come home the cards are stacked against them.... it's a tough time. Some of come out with a certificate from prison for running a forklift or obtain a GED, but it's all useless if you cannot get hired because you are a felon and tagged for life, no one will touch you. We need reform and it needs to come from you as a victim of a system that is not working.

Feel free to contact me, Spanky Macher at spankymacher@gmail.com, if you would like me to speak to your group or help you while you are on this journey.

The Target Letter Sent to Me by The Government- OH MAN!!!

I cannot help but to think about how hard it's been to go through the past 10 years. First, my life's dedication and work slowly started slipping away from my fingertips. Those restaurants were my sweat, blood, and tears. My brother, Richard, took Macados. My mother, who was to transfer to her stock to me for my success with company, decided unbeknownst to me, that she had other plans. All of those years of hard work and loyalty went straight down the drain in almost no time. It devastated me. It was like watching my own horror story as I watched Richard and mother rape Spanky's financially. They kept making really bad decisions, leading to closing many of the locations. I attempted to keep them going and opened up a few new locations in hopes that one of these would be the star and this solution would save us all.

It could have worked, but the external factors kept growing and were never resolved. Richard just kept the momentum rolling and to top it off, he had Mother wrapped around his pinky. He had a way with convincing our mother into making poor decisions that was affecting all of us.

Have you ever tried swimming across the river with your hands tied behind your back? You can't do it, I've tried multiple times, but it was just fruitless, instead I lost a lot valuable time in my life treading water.

It was the saddest day of my life when I had to report to prison for tax evasion. Thank you, Mother, who was dying in 2009, the government doesn't want you, it's not worth it for them to incarcerate an 80-year-old woman. Richard and Margaret received immunity for testifying against me. I was more than mortified. Instead, I pulled on my bootstraps, and did my time. This was not a badge of honor, nor was it a sign of success.

I came home, just like many other inmates pulling their time, and had to rebuild my life. It took a few years, but I did it. When you take small steps, breathe daily, and put one block on top of another, you can do it, and that's what I did. I was used to living in an 8x10 space with a desk top and a locker, so moving to a small townhouse was like being in heaven. I realized how happy I am with much less than before I went to camp. I realized that material items can be replaced, but you can't replace your family. You can't replace the mutual love you have. I saw this experience as one that I had to accept responsibility for. I did this, even though I really wasn't guilty...I've always taught my children that it's highly important to accept the responsibility of their actions. When this happens, you become a better person.

I decided to stay in the real estate business, wrote a book, "Slumlord Millionaire", which is about whether you can and get into buying and selling property. I was doing well with this and have a nice portfolio built up for my children.

Needless to say, I've had multiple learning experiences while managing tenants. The next thing I know is that a 6-inch binder was being provided to the US Attorney, who was investigating me for mail fraud. Unbelievable. I was advised to get an attorney. Not again! I don't have another $50k laying around, especially for a witch hunt. I applied for legal assistance and was granted it for to obtain a local attorney.

Bottom line was that once again, I was being singled out and targeted by my local government and this was sent up the ladder. Fortunately for me, the judge who was on the case, could not find anything to charge me with and the charges were dropped.

Your nightmare may never go away. You have many sleepless nights. You wonder who the person in the dark suit is standing at the corner. You wonder who is hiding in the trees, or if your phone is being tapped. You become very cautious. You don't even want to step off the curb the wrong way. You drive the speed limit. When you sneeze, you apologize, you are always looking over your shoulder, wondering what's next, what's going to happen, and what do I need to stay safe and sound.

Enjoy your freedom.

Chester the Cockroach
I would like to share this fun story at the close of this book.

I met Chester is a prison camp kitchen in the summer of 2012.

My name is Robinhood, or at least that's what they call me in the big house. I guess it comes from the fact that the famous Robin of Locksley and I have similar criminal profiles.

Unfortunately, for me, that's where the similarity stopped. As many of us know, his ending got him Lady Marion, in mine, I got life. It's understandable, he robbed the rich and gave to the poor. I robbed from everyone, and kept it all.

Anyway, one morning, while working in the prison camp kitchen, I lifted a large plastic bag of trash out of a circular, galvanized can, better known as a garbage receptacle. Guess what I found? Six cockroaches at the bottom, screaming for their very lives. There was no place to hide!

Please understand that in prison cockroaches are a part of the system. To a convict, a cockroach is like a pair of socks, a pair of shoes or the very jumpsuit he wears. Cockroaches are almost issued to convicts. They outnumber convicts 50-1. No lie.

Roaches love prisons. It's dirty, some inmates seldom shower, and the food is very "used and reachable". In particular, cockroaches love "death row", where the residents typically live alone for years. These convicts are all desperate for just one true friend, someone to talk to as they patiently wait for their personal end of time. Death row is where the older, wiser, and more experienced cockroaches hang out. There is always plenty to eat, someone who cares, and all the comforts of home.

In prison, there are typically only three things you can do with a cockroach. You can kill him, feed him, or put him to work, because in prison, everyone works. In my day, I killed one cockroach, fed one, and put two to work. The rest, I avoided.

The one I killed had a bad attitude. He pooped in my toothbrush. The one I fed convinced me he would work for food. He was a liar. After I fed him one morning, he was cleaning up around the toilet bowl when suddenly he flushed himself down and headed for the beach…to the water and the good life. The two that I put to work had families to support. I guess I'm just an old softie.

So here I am, looking down on six roaches screaming and scrambling around to save their own lives. "Please don't kill me". "I'll provide sexual favors". "I'll do anything you want". On and on it went, as each tried to climb up the side of the can only to have me send him back to a fate I controlled. This was the only time in prison that I could control anything. I was enjoying that moment.

All of these roaches were in a state of panic, that is, all but one. He sat motionless and said nothing, as his five friends continued to win my favor. Ah, the power!

I studied the situation before me and listened to the drama for a few minutes as it continued to unfold. I could take it no longer. I leaned over and placed my forefinger on the bottom of the empty can directly in front of the motionless roach. He very slowly climbed aboard and I lifted him to safety, as he sat on quietly on my fingernail. With my other hand, I reached for the can of prison bug spray which consists of Tobacco sauce and apple cider vinegar and freely sprayed the other five. Their scurrying intensified but only for a few more seconds. Then all was quiet. The five were dead.

I brought the lone survivor, still sitting on my fingernail, toward my face. He motioned me closer and whispered, "My name is Chester and I am dying from food poison. You saved me in vain".

Those were Chester's last words. With that, he turned over on his back and was no more. I checked his pulse. There was none. For some unknown reason, I felt a chill. It was a sad moment for me.

I found a Pillsbury Dough Boy dinner roll, half eaten in the bag of garbage. I pulled it from the can, separated the top from the bottom and gently laid Chester to rest. I carefully closed the roll into a sandwich and placed it inside the large bag of waste before me. I then placed it atop all the other bags of garbage. Head down, I walked back inside and continued working, acting as if nothing bad had happened.

But then, something did happen! I learned a profound lesson. At one time, I made a promise to myself, and I have lived by that promise ever since. From that day on, whenever I saw a cockroach, I went out of my way.......to kill the little bastard. I even planned cockroach safaris that took place in the middle of the night. I would turn off the lights for ten minutes, just enough time for all the roaches to think it was safe to come out of hiding. Then, I would dramatically flip on the light switch and start stomping the "shit outta dem". Of course, I wore shoes. I even went as far as wearing shoes on my hands. I bounced around the room like a rubber dog, stomping and screaming, screaming and stomping.

That picturesque setting lasted for one month, exactly. It was then that they took me away in a white jacket, that was literally strapped to my body, but no handcuffs or shackles. Now I sit alone, on a concrete floor of an empty room, still somewhere in the bowels of the prison system.

I watch! I wait! I hope! Anticipating just one more cockroach. I want to make amends. I want somebody to talk to. I need a friend...even if it's just a cockroach.

The moral of this story is not complicated. What's a deplorable bug to many, serves a purpose for others. One never knows if, and/or when, one of many becomes one of the few...

The End.

Biography

Roland "Spanky" Macher was born in Hackensack, NJ, but grew up in Wayne, NJ. Out-of-the-womb, self-made entrepreneur extraordinaire, Spanky's business adventures started at an early age delivering vegetables to our neighbors. He was never without a job or had his hands in something. Spanky moved to Virginia with his family and graduated from Madison College. It was shortly after graduation when Spanky got involved in the restaurant business. The first store was a huge success and other locations soon popped up as doors of opportunity kept growing.

Spanky's main priority was to make sure he provided a loving home and comfortable lifestyle for his family. Based on his blueprint for success, he was able to make that happen. Spanky, learning as he's going along, unfortunately makes some clearly poor decisions that leads him into a USP Camp in Hazelton, West Virginia. While he served his time, he took some time for self-reflection and poured himself into his writings. He wrote this book to share his story, experiences, and provide some insight on what to expect should you find yourself a "Deer Caught in the Headlights".

Once Spanky completed his time with the Feds, he came home to nothing, EXCEPT, a new opportunity to start over. He had a renewed sense of gratitude and appreciation for his children. He takes responsibility for his actions and since his release he's been working on projects that essentially help others.